Living Together and the Law
A Guide to Cohabitation

By David Cobern

ORHE
MEDIA LTD

The Family Law Co.
by Hartnell Chanot

First published in 2016 by:
RHE Media Ltd
5 Pennsylvania Crescent
Exeter
EX4 4SF
www.wordstothewise.co.uk

ISBN 9781910226483 (Paperback)
ISBN 9781910226469 (eBook-Kindle)
ISBN 9781910226476 (eBook-ePub)

Disclaimer: This publication is a statement of general legal principles and is not intended to be treated as formal legal advice about an individual reader's particular circumstances. Legal advice is fact-sensitive and everyone's situation differs. Therefore readers should seek legal advice that is relevant to their particular situation.

British Library Cataloguing in Publication Data
A catalogue record for this book is available from the British Library.

Printed in the UK by: Printondemand-worldwide.com, 9 Culley Court, Orton Southgate, Peterborough, PE2 6XD

RHE
MEDIA LTD
www.wordstothewise.co.uk

The Family Law Co. by Hartnell Chanot
www.thefamilylawco.co.uk

Contents

Resources:

Foreword

If one was to go into any cafe, pub, supermarket, doctor's waiting room or member's club across England and Wales, and was to ask people what they thought about the rules regarding cohabitation without marriage, I guarantee that the vast majority of them would still, to this day, talk about the 'common law wife' (or husband) which, as all lawyers know, is a complete myth, particularly in relation to property rights.

This is despite the huge publicity over the potential for a new law to govern this situation being raised by the Law Commission in 2007 and abandoned by the Labour government in 2008 and by the Coalition government in 2011. Inheritance rights were similarly addressed by the Law Commission in 2011 and not acted upon by the government. There is yet another briefing paper on the subject dated February 2016.

But that does not mean that the current legal position should not be widely understood by people who are involved in such relationships and their families.

In light of the foregoing, the need for a clearly written, practical, but legally correct, text in this area of the law that is concise, approachable and understandable is obvious. The misunderstandings, preconceptions and uncertainties of most lay-people in this area go beyond property rights, and encompass children, parental responsibility and inheritance.

It is so refreshing to see that David has managed to produce a text that complies so with the requirements set out in the paragraph above, and is of a size that should not be daunting to even the most timid of readers. It covers the important areas in such a practical manner that I expect that many lawyers practising in this area will keep a copy of the book hidden behind their weighty tomes of 'proper' law texts!

The book is organised in a clear and logical manner which reflects David's no-nonsense but friendly approach to clients that I have experienced over nearly 30 years of working with him. He is one of the most thorough, thoughtful and practical members of the legal profession that I know, and I am honoured that he asked me to write this foreword and am extremely pleased to recommend this book to everyone who needs an approachable and accurate guide to this area of the law.

Michael Berkley, Joint Head of Chambers, Magdalen Chambers and Civil Recorder

The Family Law Company

Some 25 years ago an idea for a new kind of specialist Family Law practice was born of a realisation that, in relation to the way the law then commonly operated, it actually made matters far worse for families in difficulty. What was needed was a problem-solving approach based on sound principles that put the interests of any children at the centre of the negotiations. There had to be a better way, a way in which law could be put to work FOR individuals to resolve their differences with the minimum of stress, delay, polarised positions and cost. This was to be a respectful and humane way of meeting people at their point of need, helping them to find solutions and involving them fully in regaining control of their lives in situations where they had felt out of control.

The Family Law Company by Hartnell Chanot grew from that initial idea, with a determination to serve clients' needs (not those of the lawyers), and to involve clients fully in finding solutions by helping them understand clearly how the law could help their situation whatever that might be, for both privately paying clients and for those who need legal aid.

Over time the company has grown from four staff, including its founder Norman Hartnell, to its present tally of some 70 employees specialising in the whole range of family problems including those of an ever-growing unmarried population. Norman was initially joined by Jane Chanot who shares his vision, and they have invited equally devoted and like-minded lawyers to join them as owners of the company to drive the business forward. Having started from a small office in 1991 in Castle St., Exeter, the company now occupies some 12,000 square feet of offices in Exeter and in Plymouth opposite the Family Courts, and it also has outposts elsewhere in the South West. The Family Law Company remains committed to the vision of putting law to work for those in need.

Specialist teams have been formed to deal with such diverse matters as: the resolution of issues concerning financial and children matters arising from a couple's separation; representation of children and parents in care proceedings; international abduction; protection of the victims of domestic abuse; mediation and other alternative dispute resolution models.

David Cobern, one of the company's owners, leads our team who advise those who are leaving an unmarried relationship. The law in this area is complex and very different to that applying when couples have been married. He draws on his wealth of legal and practical experience in this book, which answers the real questions he is commonly asked as he highlights traps for the unwary and explodes some myths in a style that is easy to read and understand. You could not be in better hands if you are looking for clear guidance in this area. It is my hope that in its pages you will find answers to your own personal questions and have a clearer understanding of how the law can help you.

Norman Hartnell
Managing Director

Acknowledgements

The author would like to thank the following people for their contributions to this book:

Dale Simpson, FCA CTA at Thomas Westcott Accountants Exeter. Dale is a Chartered Accountant and Tax Advisor, he has been a Partner at Thomas Westcott since 2007 and is based in our Exeter office. As a practicing member of the Academy of Experts and the Expert Witness Institute, Dale spends much of his time providing evidence in the Courts as an expert witness in cases concerning matrimonial proceedings, personal injury/medical negligence claims, business disputes and professional negligence. 'Aside from my work as an expert witness, I also provide share valuations in cases of business succession and the purchase or sale of businesses'. Dale also lectures on accountancy and taxation matters to professional bodies and is chairman of the South West of England branch of the Chartered Institute of Taxation. In his spare time, Dale is a keen motorsports enthusiast. See more at: **https://www.thomaswestcott.co.uk/about-the-firm/our-people/8-partners/13-dale-simpson#sthash.xTEjjg4A.dpuf**

Eliana Sydes, FPFS Specialist in financial planning during divorce and separation at Towry Wealth advisers, Exeter.

Ian Walker, Partner specialising in Business rescue and recovery at Begbies Traynor Insolvency Practitioners. Ian joined Begbies in 2000 from Pannell Kerr Forster after practicing insolvency for the previous 20 years with Big Four firms. A member of R3 and a Fellow of the Institute of Chartered Accountants in England and Wales (from which he also takes his Insolvency Licence), he is currently a member of the ICAEW Investigation Committee. Over the years, Ian has dealt with all types of insolvency and at least three recessions. Currently, his practice based in Exeter and Plymouth covers the whole of Devon and Cornwall (including the Scilly Isles), together with as much of Somerset and Dorset as he can get away with! He deals with all types of personal and corporate insolvency and also concentrates on pre- and post-lending review work for all the major lending institutions.

The author and publisher would also like to acknowledge and/or thank the following organisations for permission to reproduce their material in this book. Every attempt has been made to seek permission for the copyright material that has been used. However, if we have inadvertently used copyright material without permission/acknowledgement we apologise and we will make the necessary correction at the first opportunity.

Resource 2: Parental Responsibility Agreement - Form C(PRA1) (08.14) - http://www.justice.gov.uk/forms Contains public sector information licensed under the Open Government Licence v3.0. **http://www.nationalarchives.gov.uk/doc/open-government-licence/version/3/**

Resource 3 – Form JO - HM Land Registry Form JO © Crown copyright (ref: LR/HO) 08/15 Contains public sector information licensed under the Open Government Licence v3.0. http://www.nationalarchives.gov.uk/doc/open-government-licence/version/3/

Resource 4 – The Intestacy Rules - Taken from **https://www.citizensadvice.org.uk/relationships/death-and-wills/who-can-inherit-if-there-is-no-will-the-rules-of-intestacy/#h-what-are-the-rules-of-intestacy** Reproduced by kind permission of Citizens Advice 2016

Resource 5 – Form TR1 - HM Land Registry Form TR1 © Crown copyright (ref: LR/HO) 08/15 Contains public sector information licensed under the Open Government Licence v3.0. **http://www.nationalarchives.gov.uk/doc/open-government-licence/version/3/**

Resource 6 – Request to health professional for medical evidence of injuries/condition consistent with domestic violence - From: Legal Aid Agency. Part of: Legal aid cases of domestic violence and child abuse: letters for professionals. Published: 26 April 2014. Updated: 25 April 2016 **https://www.gov.uk/government/publications/give-evidence-of-injuries-consistent-with-domestic-violence** Contains public sector information licensed under the Open Government Licence v3.0. **http://www.nationalarchives.gov.uk/doc/open-government-licence/version/3/**

Resource 7 – Request to Social Services for evidence of an assessment of child abuse or a child protection plan - From: Legal Aid Agency. Part of: Legal aid cases of domestic violence and child abuse: letters for professionals. Published: 26 April 2014 **https://www.gov.uk/government/publications/give-evidence-of-domestic-violence-assessments-social-services-departments** Contains public sector information licensed under the Open Government Licence v3.0. **http://www.nationalarchives.gov.uk/doc/open-government-licence/version/3/**

Resource 10 – Inheritance Tax and Settled Property - From: HM Revenue & Customs. Published: 8 November 2010. Updated: 6 April 2016. Rates, allowances and duties have been updated for the tax year 2016 to 2017. **https://www.gov.uk/guidance/trusts-and-inheritance-tax** Contains public sector information licensed under the Open Government Licence v3.0. **http://www.nationalarchives.gov.uk/doc/open-government-licence/version/3/**

PART I

OVERVIEW

Life is what happens to us while we are making other plans.

(*Allen Saunders, Publishers Syndicate.*)

Introduction

This is not intended to be a dry legal textbook (although parts of it necessarily are). It represents my long experience working for (and now as a director of) a firm of family law specialists and my particular interest in the legal rights and issues affecting unmarried couples. This is not about obscure points of law, but the practical legal and financial issues that arise time and again for unmarried couples during their relationships and on separation or death. It provides readily understandable information about protective measures and remedies available to people contemplating, already in, or emerging from, unmarried cohabitation. Whichever category you fall into, my hope is that you will find it helpful and informative.

We lawyers deal with cold, hard facts. We are paid to ask 'What if?' Consequently, this book will be anathema to the incurable romantic. I make no apology for that. It is intended to help those who want to know and 'hats off' to those who feel able to trust to luck. I hope it works out for you. If you believe that you and your partner may not be attuned to one another's feelings about these issues, then you may feel this is not a work to share with them or indeed to keep on your bedside table.

COHABITATION DEFINED

> To live together and have a sexual relationship without being married.[1]

The legal statutory definition:

> A man and a woman who are (or were) living together as if they were husband and wife; or
> Two persons of the same sex who are (or were) living together as if they were civil partners.[2]

More couples are choosing to live together outside marriage. In 2015, out of a total of 18.7 million families living in the UK, 12.5 million consisted of married couples (including same sex married/civil partnerships) and 3.2 million families included unmarried couples.

This is compared with just 2.1 million cohabiting unmarried couples in 2000. Very significantly, cohabitation appears to have reached a tipping point in terms of social acceptability so that it is moving swiftly from rare to commonplace and in due course, if present trends continue, to the norm. To illustrate the pace of change, the number of people who were cohabiting with one another in the 1980s was a fraction of the number doing so now. Between 2000 and 2010 the number of children living in opposite sex cohabiting families increased from 1.3 million to 1.8 million (an increase of over 38 per cent).

Over the last three decades there have been developments in the law affecting the unmarried. Unmarried fathers can now acquire parental responsibility for their children by being present at the registration of the birth rather than having to seek a court order or written agreement.[3] Unmarried couples have been recognised as potentially providing a stable and loving relationship into which children can now be legally adopted.[4] Limited rights have been introduced for unmarried partners who are financially dependent on their partner to claim against the partner's estate on death.[5]

However, popular misconceptions remain. In fact the above developments have contributed to this. Many couples in long-term unmarried relationships mistakenly believe they enjoy rights akin to their married counterparts. Some cohabitees think of themselves as the 'common law spouse'. Calling oneself a 'common law spouse' might, to the more conservative minded, carry some significance in terms of respectability, but it is no more than a self-appointed 'label' to which no legal rights attach whatsoever. The lack of awareness is sufficiently widespread that the Ministry of Justice has funded two voluntary sector partners[6] to manage a campaign to make cohabitants more aware of their legal status and to provide them with practical advice on how they can protect themselves and their families, should they wish to do so.

NOTES

[1] The *Oxford English Dictionary* definition.

[2] S25 Family Law (Scotland) Act 2006.

[3] Children Act 1989 s.4 (1) (a) refers.

[4] Adoption and Children Act 2002 S48 (1) refers.

[5] Law Reform (Succession) Act 1995 inserting S1A and S1B to the Inheritance (Provision for Family and Dependents) Act 1975.

[6] **http://www.advicenow.org.uk/a-to-z/c#browseAZ** and **http://www.oneplusone.org.uk/**

◆1◆

Just a Piece of Paper?

WHAT IS THE DIFFERENCE BETWEEN BEING MARRIED AND UNMARRIED?

Here is a familiar quote:

> I John take you, Jane,
> to be my wife,
> to have and to hold
> from this day forward;
> for better, for worse,
> for richer, for poorer,
> in sickness and in health,
> to love and to cherish,
> till death us do part;
> according to God's holy law.
> In the presence of God I make this vow
>
> Jane, I give you this ring as a sign of our marriage.
> With my body I honour you,
> all that I am I give to you,
> and all that I have I share with you,
> within the love of God,
> Father, Son and Holy Spirit.[7]

They are beautiful and momentous words. Whatever you think about marriage as an institution, the meaning of the marriage vow is clear. The couple openly promise to stick with one other through thick and thin for the rest of their lives and to share all that they have. While some unmarried couples may make informal promises to one another, there is no legal significance to this and many more couples make no promises at all. They are free to separate at any time without legal repercussions.

There are some legal implications in relation to the arrangements for unmarried parents and their children (dealt with later), but the really significant practical and legal differences lie in the approach to financial arrangements on separation.

From a legal perspective the promise made by a married couple makes the task of deciding how to deal with their financial arrangements simpler on separation. This is reflected in the act of parliament that gives the courts powers to decide these things. It is known as The Matrimonial Causes Act 1973.[8] It gives judges a clear set of guidelines. It requires them to take into account things like:

- the needs of the children;
- what each spouse earns;
- how much capital they each have;
- what they each need;
- whether either of them has health problems;
- how long they have been married;
- what standard of living they have enjoyed together;
- what they have each contributed;
- whether either of them has behaved very badly;
- what benefits either of them would lose when the marriage ends (for example, pension rights).

Regardless of who owns property, savings or pension rights, or who generates the income in a marriage, the court can adjust it to produce a fair result. Lots of case law (previous decisions) has been created to help judges interpret the rules. Consequently lawyers are able to advise their married clients of the range of possible outcomes with a fair degree of accuracy.

To give effect to their decisions the divorce courts have the powers they need. They can adjust shares in marital property (regardless of which spouse is the legal owner at the end of the marriage). They can make maintenance orders, lump sum orders and share out pension rights.

For the unmarried, fairness is irrelevant to the outcome. The court cannot take into account any of the things referred to in the list above when deciding how to settle their financial arrangements. Neither can the court:

- adjust shares in property;
- make a maintenance order for one partner against the other; [9]
- make lump sum orders for one partner against the other; [10]
- share pensions.

So, for example, a judge cannot:

- Order an unmarried man to transfer some of his share in a jointly owned property to his former partner because she is earning less and cannot borrow enough to purchase a home of her own.[11]
- Order the high earning former cohabitee of an unemployed, disabled woman to pay maintenance to her.[12]
- Order a wealthy banker to pay a lump sum to his former unmarried partner who has no savings of her own.[13]
- Order an unmarried fireman with a generous pension to share it with the mother of his children even though she might have sacrificed career aspirations to look after them.

WHY DOES THIS DIFFERENCE SOMETIMES CREATE PROBLEMS FOR UNMARRIED COUPLES?

The commonest cause of dispute in unmarried relationships is differing expectations combined with reluctance to address 'the elephant in the room'. 'Maybe our relationship will end or be damaged if I ask the question that is troubling me.' For some, not asking is a risk worth taking and so the couple proceed at cross-purposes. Some labour for years under the illusion that their partner shares their view about what should happen financially if they separate.

Consequently, separation after a committed relationship can have catastrophic consequences for one party. The most extreme situations will see the person who owns none of the assets left virtually penniless after a long relationship because their partner owns all the assets and offers no financial provision whatsoever.

There are remedies available for financial provision for children, but one partner often finds themselves left out in the cold financially.

Irrespective of what may be said after a relationship ends, we have all felt moved to give assurances to our partners about our love for them and our shared plans for the future. In hindsight, these conversations are often interpreted differently. For example, 'I vaguely remember saying this was to be your home for life before you moved to live with me. But that was ages ago and I remember a few months ago you said you knew it was my house and you have no right to stay here'. When it comes to their day in court people will almost always have conflicting recollections about what was said between them and which conversations actually mattered.

If the couple end up in court, the court's findings about these frequently vague and historic recollections will determine the very uncertain outcome of litigation between them. It all too often comes down to the performance of the witness on the stand; a terrible way to decide something that could have been agreed in better times.

In court cases between the unmarried, where there has been no clarity or agreement, the present law requires detailed (and costly) examination of past dealings between the parties. Ironically, this defeats the very object that motivates many cohabiting couples who reject the idea of marriage -'Let's keep it simple by staying unmarried'.

Whether we choose to confront these difficult issues or not, as time passes in any relationship financial security becomes ever more important. It must be helpful for unmarried partners to be clear about what will happen if their relationship ends or on the death of one of them. This allays anxiety about the future or suspicion and misunderstanding about the other's intentions. Fairness avoids dispute, but so too does clarity. In some respects, clarity is most important, because it helps us to make the right decision about our future. If someone is wondering whether their relationship will last or whether to have a child with their partner, clarity about the financial arrangements between them will help them to make the right decision, not only for themselves, but also for their partner and (ultimately) any children.

At the end of the day, if the answer is that one unmarried partner doesn't want to share assets with the other, even though they are expecting their partner to make sacrifices for the relationship (by, for example, giving up job opportunities for children or supporting their partner's business), then the disadvantaged partner commits to the relationship at their own risk.

We lawyers strongly advocate discussions about these issues between unmarried partners. Granted, it is not a romantic proposition but, if you can reach an understanding, so much the better for all concerned. At least you won't end up lining the lawyers' pockets.

There are many different situations in which unmarried couples may want to understand their respective financial positions in their relationship:

- at the outset of the relationship (very sensible, but perhaps optimistic);
- when deciding to buy property together;
- when planning or expecting a child;
- when going into business together;
- when one party is about to introduce capital (for example, an inheritance);
- when illness strikes;
- when the relationship is ending or has ended (see Chapter 16).

NOTES

[7] From the Church of England marriage service.

[8] Section 25 a) to h) refers.

[9] Child maintenance is still available (see Chapter 17).

[10] Lump sums are available for children (see Chapter 17).

[11] The exception is a transfer for the benefit of children – but the property reverts to the payer later (more on this in Chapter 17).

[12] As above, in limited circumstances a court can order maintenance for children (more on this in Chapter 17).

[13] As above, a court can order a lump sum for child related expenses (more on this in Chapter 17).

PART II

COHABITEES AND THEIR CHILDREN

◆2◆

Parental Responsibility

Parental Responsibility (PR) is a significant concept for the unmarried couple, particularly the father. It is the legal term that describes all the rights, duties, powers and obligations that a parent has in relation to a child. It includes the right to make or to be consulted about decisions regarding a child's upbringing and welfare. A child's mother will always acquire PR from the moment of her child's birth, as will a married father. An unmarried father will only acquire PR if he is present at the office of the Registrar of Births, Deaths and Marriages when his child's birth is registered[14] (in which case he will be named on the birth certificate), or if he later marries the child's mother.

SO WHAT DOES PR MEAN AND DOES IT REALLY MATTER IF I DON'T HAVE IT?

For many the answer to these questions is 'not much' and 'no' respectively. If you are in a loving relationship and support one another, then having or not having PR appears to be of no real practical significance on a day-to-day basis. However, there are some situations for a committed unmarried father where having or not having PR does assume real (potentially life-changing) significance. To those in a settled relationship, it may seem inconceivable that you wouldn't share with each other the task of making the big decisions about your child's upbringing. By big decisions I mean things like:

- which school he or she will attend;
- whether he or she should undergo a particular course of medical or dental treatment;
- naming him or her or changing his or her name;
- removing him or her from the jurisdiction;
- decisions about his or her religious upbringing.

There are therefore sometimes unforeseen implications of not having PR.

- If a parent with PR chooses to appoint a Guardian for their child by making a will, the guardianship appointment will take effect on their death, unless there is another person with PR surviving that parent at the date of their death. This means that an unmarried father can find himself in competition with some third party (possibly unrelated to his child) to assume primary care of his child on the mother's death rather than being the obvious first choice of carer.
- On separation, a father without PR can find himself side-lined because he has no right to participate in big decisions about his child.
- Schools will routinely ask separated fathers whether they have PR to establish whether they can or should release information about the child.
- Separated fathers are regularly asked whether they have PR and can make decisions about or consent to medical treatment when presenting their child at A&E or the doctor's surgery with some injury sustained during a contact visit.
- A father without PR cannot object to the other parent removing their child from the jurisdiction or expect to be consulted as of right if their child is placed for adoption.

Thus far I have only referred to PR in terms of rights. However, as the name implies, it also entails the acceptance of responsibility for your child. Responsibility for his or her physical, emotional and general developmental welfare, including but not limited to the responsibility to financially maintain him or her. Note, however, that not having PR does not remove the obligation to financially maintain your child.

Not having PR also does not prevent a parent seeking other court orders about his child such as a Child Arrangements Order that defines how much time the child spends with him.

I AM A MOTHER EXPECTING A CHILD BY MY UNMARRIED PARTNER – SHOULD I AGREE TO HIM HAVING PR?

Of course – if you trust and support one another. However, for some mothers, the question of whether to agree to their baby's father acquiring PR at registration of the birth is a big issue. PR can be exercised responsibly and cooperatively, but it can also be exercised in a destructive and divisive manner post separation. If you are an expectant mum and your instincts are telling you to be cautious, remember that once dad is registered as your baby's father by being present at the registration of the birth this cannot be undone. You can always enter into a PR agreement with dad later if you feel it is appropriate (see below). I suppose you might ask yourself whether agreeing to dad acquiring PR for a quiet life or in the hope that he will act 'responsibly' is actually going to encourage him to do so. The proof of the pudding, as they say, is in the eating.

I AM AN UNMARRIED FATHER WITHOUT PARENTAL RESPONSIBILITY - HOW CAN I ACQUIRE IT?

There are six methods.

1. **Agreement**
You can enter into a Parental Responsibility Agreement,[15] which would then be signed by you and lodged with the Principal Registry of the Family Division in London.
2. **Court Order**
Alternatively, if the person with PR won't agree, you can make an application to the court for PR. You will need to prove that contact is taking place regularly and that there is a sufficient level of commitment by you towards your child. The court will always base its decision on what it considers to be the best interests of the child. PR Orders come to an end when the child is 18.
3. **Through a Child Arrangements Order or Special Guardianship Order.**

If you are granted a Child Arrangements Order, which says that the child shall live with you, or if you have a Special Guardianship Order, or if the parent with care passes away and you are named in their will as the guardian of the child. If you are not a father, second female parent or step-parent, the easiest way for you to acquire PR for a child is under a Child Arrangements Order that says that the child lives with you (this Order may also say that the child lives with another person - it does not have to only name one person).

4. **Marrying your child's mother.**
5. **Being appointed as the child's guardian, or**
6. **Adopting your child.**

NOTES

[14] Since 1st December 2003 courtesy of the Adoption and Children Act 2002, s.111 which amended the Children Act 1989.

[15] Resource 2.

◆3◆

Adoption of Children by Unmarried Couples

It is now possible for unmarried couples (over 21 years of age) to apply for an adoption order in relation to a child. The child must be under the age of 18 when the adoption application is made and must not be married or in a civil partnership. (At the time of going to press (June 2016) there is a plan for a Child and Social Work Bill, the aim of which is to make adoption a more viable option.)

Both birth parents normally have to agree to the adoption, unless they can't be found, are incapable of giving consent or if the child's welfare requires that they should be adopted.

While it is not necessary for the proposed adoptive parents to be British citizens, they (or one of them) must have had a fixed, permanent home in the United Kingdom for at least the last year.

To adopt a child a couple can go through an adoption agency connected to their local council or a voluntary adoption agency who will assist them through the approval process, which normally lasts for around six months before the couple are matched with a child. The process followed by the agency is as follows.

- You will be invited to preparation classes, normally local to you, and you will receive advice on the effect adoption may have on you.
- A social worker will visit you several times to carry out an assessment to find out whether you are suitable to become an adoptive parent.
- Police checks will be carried out. You will not be allowed to adopt if you, or an adult member of your family, have been convicted of a serious offence, particularly if it was an offence against a child.
- You will be asked to provide three referees who will give you a personal reference. One referee can be a relative.
- You will be asked to undergo a full medical examination.

Once the assessment has been completed, it will be sent to an independent adoption panel consisting of a group of people experienced in adoption who will make a recommendation to the adoption agency. You are permitted to attend the assessment panel's deliberations to ask questions and answer any questions they may have. The recommendation is then sent to the agency, which will then decide whether you are suitable to adopt a child.

If the answer is 'yes' the agency will begin the process of finding a child for you to adopt through either the Adoption Register for England or the National Adoption Service for Wales that hold details of children across England and Wales who need adopting.

If the answer is 'no', you can either challenge the agency's decision by writing to them or by applying to the Independent Review Mechanism, which will look into your case. Alternatively, you can still contact other adoption agencies, but that will involve starting the process again.

To make an adoption legal, you need to apply for an adoption order from the court. This will give you parental rights and responsibilities for the child.

At the date of the application, the child must have lived with you for at least ten weeks.

When an order is granted, the adoption becomes permanent. You will receive an adoption certificate showing your adopted child's new name which replaces the original birth certificate. Your adopted child has the same rights as if they were your own birth child such as, for example, the right of inheritance.

An adoption order takes away parental responsibility from the child's birth parent(s) and from anyone else who has parental responsibility for the child.

The process tends to be simpler and the chances of successfully obtaining an adoption order are greater where the child concerned is already living with the prospective adopters. This is often the case where the child is related to one of the parties, possibly his or her child by a previous relationship or where the child has been placed with the prospective adopters as part of a fostering arrangement, in which case they will already have been through the assessment process.

PART III

COHABITEES AND THEIR FINANCES

◆4◆

Property

It would be naïve to assume that everyone approaches property issues at the same point in a relationship. The question often arises for the first time on inheritance, house purchase or re-mortgage of a property already owned by one party when the other's credit rating is needed to borrow.

It is not uncommon to find relationships where the couple have settled down, maybe even with children, and one party holds all or most of the assets and earns most of the income. Inevitably the other will at times feel insecure and vulnerable. They have committed to one another in all senses except financially. This presents a problem. One partner is going to be afraid to raise an issue that might cause them to appear motivated by money or even to appear to be thinking of ending the relationship. The other party is going to be worried about opening the flood gates to the sharing of income or assets that they may be reluctant to share. So what is the best way to approach this?

Remember firstly and most importantly, whether you are the partner with or without the assets, it isn't all about what you want for yourself. If you portray it in these simplistic terms, your partner may feel threatened. Here are some tips on how to approach the subject. This is written as if it applies to the non-owning partner, but it applies every bit as much to the partner with the assets who is open to the idea of their partner acquiring a share but wanting to protect an existing contribution.

- Consider your situation carefully from the point of view of both you and your partner. Ask yourself what they are likely to want for themselves.
- It's a big subject. Don't try to tackle it all in one go. Consider breaking it down in stages.
- Read the sections of this book dealing with inheritance and pension nominations (Chapters 12 and 22). Bluntly, it is easier for a reluctant or anxious partner to make provision for dependents on death than to share assets in life. Approaching the subject in this way sets the right scene.
- Find out the cost of life insurance cover for both of you (for the same reasons and also because it is surprisingly cheap).
- If there is a property and you are worried about not having a share in it, read the rest of this chapter and Chapter 6 concerning the protection of shares in property by declaration of trust and think about what your partner will want to protect.
- If there is a business run by your partner and you want some security within it, read the section of this book dealing with business assets and taxation (Chapter 10).
- Choose your moment carefully (seriously, choose it carefully!) and approach the subject as a shared problem. Be positive and optimistic. Tell your partner about your fears for your own security and that of your children (if you have any or want to have any). Present a solution that will recognise and protect your partner's contributions, whether in terms of capital introduced to property or existing business assets, while giving you an opportunity to begin to acquire something for yourself. If you feel that you have already acquired some 'share' through your efforts, be prepared to negotiate for the sake of achieving certainty. Certainty is worth more than a 'potential future claim'.
- Offer to enter into an agreement that recognises your partner's share, but gives you something approximating what you have invested and/or an opportunity to begin to acquire an interest (for example, through contributing to a mortgage on the home you share or working in a business). It is preferable to present this as part of measures ensuring provision for you both and for your child(ren) in the event of death or illness rather what would happen if you were to separate. Don't

forget to emphasise the potential benefits for each of you in in terms of taxation.

What if you are the partner with all or most of the assets? Would you be prepared to share future gains with your partner if you could be reassured that in doing so you wouldn't be giving up the hard-earned assets that you brought to the relationship? Or do you accept that your partner has already made a significant contribution that ought to be recognised? Consider what your partner might be thinking about their situation and what might reassure them for the future. Consider the above points from your perspective and what you would expect in return for offering your partner the opportunity to acquire or begin to acquire a financial stake in the assets and income.

THE HOUSE BUYING PROCESS – WHAT NORMALLY HAPPENS?

When you buy a home together you will have to think about how to raise the purchase price. The shared excitement of finding and buying your first home together often causes one or both of you to overlook the obvious. The pressing concern is to find the right house and then the necessary money by whatever means, often with surprisingly little thought for where it comes from. The stress of trying to secure the home you have chosen against other interested buyers, raising a mortgage and a myriad other details right down to the décor and booking the removal van takes priority. In many cases the financial arrangements are not revisited except on separation, at which point recriminations frequently ensue over who contributed what and when.

In the typical house purchase, the question of shares in your new home will be discussed only briefly, if at all. These days you will probably be collared by your estate agent trying to persuade you to instruct a solicitor hundreds of miles away to deal with your purchase. Many people will never meet the person who will handle the single biggest transaction in their lives, let alone discuss shares in the property with them. Even a local high street conveyancing solicitor facing market pressures and handling many transactions every week may be reluctant to prompt a face-to-face conversation with clients about their shares in the home. This is a topic that may have been given little thought in the whirl of house hunting. Even if he does ask the question, the chances are he won't be thanked by his clients for asking them without warning to consider a subject they may have avoided. Many people prefer to put such a difficult subject out of their minds and proceed 'on trust' with their partner.

Just recently I came across a woman whose parents provided a deposit of £50,000 to enable her to purchase a property jointly with her partner. When a thorough conveyancing solicitor asked them if they wanted a written agreement prepared, her partner responded that he would be 'upset' if she didn't trust him, so she agreed to proceed without one. They later separated and she feared that her partner may want to claim a share of the money her parents invested; it remains to be seen whether he will....

The courts have repeatedly issued authoritative judgements encouraging the profession to address these problems by making detailed records of advice and instructions. A typical comment is one made by an exasperated Lord Justice Ward in the 2002 case of *Goodman* v. *Gallant*, when he said:

> I ask in despair how often this court has to remind conveyancers that they would save their clients a great deal of later difficulty if only they would sit the purchasers down, explain the difference between a joint tenancy and a tenancy in common, ascertain what they want and then expressly declare in the conveyance or transfer how the beneficial interest is to be held because that will be conclusive and save all argument. When are conveyancers going to do this as a matter of invariable standard practice? This court has urged that time after time. Perhaps conveyancers do not read the law reports. I will try one more time: ALWAYS TRY TO AGREE ON AND THEN RECORD HOW THE BENEFICIAL INTEREST IS TO BE HELD. It is not very difficult to do.[16]

This has been taken up by the Law Society in good practice guidance to the profession[17] and the Land Registry by the introduction of a voluntary form JO[18].

Some solicitors have tried to follow this guidance. In a fixed fee conveyance this can be an uphill struggle. Here is one such exchange between a solicitor and client quoted by the judge in the landmark 2004 case of *Oxley* v. *Hiscock*. The solicitor (after previous attempts to obtain instructions) wrote to Ms Oxley:

> It is essential for me to have your written instructions as to how you wish me to deal with the proceeds of sale [of 39 Page Close]. I think you wish me to apply the whole of this sum towards the purchase of 35 Dickens Close by Mr Hiscock. If that is correct then I must have your very clear instructions in writing. You must also give very serious consideration as to whether you do wish to invest all of your net sale proceeds in the purchase of 35 Dickens Close which will be in the sole name of Mr Hiscock.

> If any dispute should then arise between yourself and Mr Hiscock in the future then you will have difficulty in establishing any claim in respect of 35 Dickens Close or any claim for a refund of the investment which you have made in that property.
> My advice must be that you should be a joint purchaser of 35 Dickens Close or that you should at least require Mr Hiscock to enter into a Trust deed to confirm that the property will be held by him on trust for both of you and such deed should also set out the respective shares to which you will each be entitled. Alternatively you could require a second mortgage to be entered in your favour against 35 Dickens Close.

Ms Oxley replied in a letter dated 23 April 1991:

> I . . . confirm that I wish all the proceeds from the sale of 39 Page Close, Brean to be put towards the purchase of 35 Dickens Close by Mr A. Hiscock.
> Your comments on any claim I might have to 35 Dickens Close have been noted, and I appreciate your concern.
> However, I am quite satisfied with the present arrangements, and feel I know Mr Hiscock well enough not to need written legal protection in this matter.

Plainly Ms Oxley did not know Mr Hiscock as well as she thought because they ended up before the highest court in the land litigating over the property at huge expense. This not untypical example illustrates the difficulty faced by the profession where time is money and a fixed price is important to the client, and where clients – often in the flush of love and excitement in purchasing a home – do not want to address the difficult question of who owns how much of that home.

The solution that the legal profession has come up with is the standard 'factsheet', one of a number that will accompany the standard conveyancing solicitor's client care letter. This vital question is given too little attention in the average house purchase. From a legal standpoint however, that doesn't matter. It was sent to you and you ought to have read it. The solicitor has done what he is professionally obliged to do.

The factsheet will set out your options to share the equity in your new home. Remember one important point - legal ownership of a property (the name of the person on the title deeds) is not the same as beneficial ownership (the value). Legally, it is possible for a person to own a property, but to hold all the value on trust for another person. A good analogy would be the government-sponsored Child Trust Fund accounts. They belong to your children, but you, as parent, are named as the account holder. You are the legal owner of the account, but you do not own the value of it. You are holding it on trust for your child. The same principle applies to property ownership - a legal owner can hold all or some of the value for someone else. When it comes to the value of the property, there are three possible forms of ownership.

1. Joint Beneficial Tenants

You own all of the property jointly with your partner. If one of you dies, his or her share passes to the survivor. Even if the partner who died left a will passing all their property and other assets to someone else, their share of the property will still pass to the surviving owner. The implication of this is that your shares are equal in life, but people rarely turn their minds to this in the context of a possible separation. Most conveyancing solicitors' advice factsheets concentrate on the survivorship point, but omit to mention that this arrangement implies equal shares on separation. This advice fulfils their professional obligation to the parties, but it does not give the whole picture – to the consternation of many on separation.

Therefore, the presumption that a court will take from this acceptance that your partner would inherit your share on your death is that you also accept they should receive an equal share on separation. It will be very difficult to overcome this presumption before a court if there is a transfer document (Resource 5 Form TR1) completed to create a joint beneficial tenancy and signed by both of you, and even if the advice about the implications was inadequate in some respects and the contributions to the purchase price were unequal. Because of the implied equality in this arrangement, a joint beneficial tenancy can be changed by either owner serving a notice of severance on the other, which then creates a Tenancy in Common in equal shares so that the survivorship rule would no longer apply and the deceased's share would not pass to the survivor (see below).

2. Tenants in Common in equal shares

The difference between Joint Beneficial Tenants and Tenants in Common is that, in the latter case, if one owner dies, their share passes to whoever is named in their will (assuming they left one) or, if there is no will, to their next of kin. This form of ownership has particular relevance if you are unmarried because you will not inherit your partner's share of your jointly owned home if your partner dies, unless they leave their share to you by a valid will (see the intestacy rules in Chapter 22 and in Resource 4). A widow(er), on the other hand, will automatically inherit their spouse's share on death even if they left no will. If you have children with your (unmarried) partner and your partner dies intestate (without a valid will), their share will pass to the children in trust until they attain majority at age 18.

3. Tenants in Common in unequal shares

This is the same as for 2. above, except that your shares are not equal. They are defined in a Deed. The shares can be percentage terms (i.e. 60:40), as fractions (i.e. 3/5ths to 2/5ths) or as a fixed interest (i.e. as to £100,000 to X and the balance to Y).

Most conveyancing solicitors will ask their clients (who have hopefully read and understood the factsheet) to tick the relevant box, then sign and return the factsheet to the solicitor as confirmation of instructions. A good solicitor will take note of the source of the deposit or purchase money (if there is no mortgage) and check whether the parties want an agreement to reflect any unequal contribution. So, for example, where one party has contributed £50,000 towards a purchase price of £150,000, with the balance raised by a mortgage, the solicitor should have a discussion with the parties about whether it is appropriate to their situation to register their shares as Joint Beneficial Tenants (if one dies, the survivor takes all and shares are effectively equal) or as Tenants in Common and, if so, in what shares. This is important because, legally speaking, from the day of completion, the way in which the shares are defined will determine division of the proceeds on sale, even if the parties were to separate within a week of completion. Would it be fair if a joint owner who contributed the whole deposit of, say, £50,000 had to share that equally with their partner when they to separate one month after completion? Clearly not, but without a written agreement to divide the shares unequally, this is the potential result.

A DECLARATION OF TRUST

A solution to the problem of recording shares in the property is an agreement (known as a Declaration of Trust) that defines the shares and that will help to prevent dispute. In its simplest form this is done by ticking a box on the standard property transfer Form TR1[19] used in all property transactions. This document has been in use since April 1998 and provides a tick box for each of the three forms of property ownership listed above. The Land Registry will insist on this form being completed in every transaction. However there are drawbacks that make this option unreliable.

- Solicitors' records of the advice given and instructions received vary enormously. Sometimes there is no record at all. Sometimes the signed factsheet is present, but one partner denies any involvement in the decision because there was never any discussion with the solicitor directly. Sometimes, the advice was simply inadequate for the parties to understand what they were being asked to confirm. However, sometimes the records of the advice and instructions are clear and comprehensive.
- In most relationships, one party tends to take responsibility for the paperwork. I often show a copy of a signed factsheet from a solicitor's conveyancing file to clients to be greeted with the comment; 'I just signed what (my partner) put in front of me. I trusted (my partner)' or '(my partner) asked me to sign this when I was tired after a busy day at work' and 'No, I never spoke directly to the solicitor'.
- The declaration freezes the parties' shares at the date of purchase. Where one party has made a contribution to the deposit and they intend that they will both contribute to the mortgage, the declaration that they own their shares unequally is not sufficiently flexible to take into account those contributions as the mortgage reduces. The tick box exercise is not sufficient and something more comprehensive is required to achieve that (more on this below).
- Extraordinarily, there is no legal requirement for purchasers to sign the TR1 transfer document unless they are entering into agreements (covenants) or indemnities to relieve the sellers of obligations relating to the property such as rights of way. Only the sellers must sign it. Many conveyancing files I have inspected contain a transfer document containing a ticked box indicating the parties' shares in the property but signed only by the sellers. Inevitably, the party who doesn't want to be bound to a particular share denies all knowledge of the arrangement and points to the absence of a signature.
- I have seen a number of instances where solicitors who don't have a written record of their clients' instructions about property shares on file have the incomplete form TR1 returned to them by the Land Registry with a request to tick the relevant box and return the form. Alarmingly, some have done so without checking with their clients.

Therefore, the problem with using form TR1 is that it is seen as very much a standard part of the transaction in every house purchase rather than something to which the parties and solicitor have expressly turned their attention to record the parties' shares in the property.

If you simply don't have the spare cash to pay for a bespoke Declaration of Trust, my tip is that you make sure you sit down together with your partner before completion and have the necessary conversation about recognising any inequality in contributions to the deposit. You should then make doubly sure when giving instructions to your conveyancing solicitor that he records your agreement and refers to it in correspondence addressed to you both, which you should then both read and acknowledge. By that method there can be no argument. Don't assume that the solicitor is doing this. It is surprising how often it either doesn't happen at all or is inadequately recorded. Don't be shy about it or intimidated by the solicitor. He is working for you and part of his role is to advise on this issue and record your agreement.

If you have any doubts ask the solicitor to ensure that he completes and submits a form 'JO'. This form will require him to obtain and record your explicit instructions on your and your partner's shares in the property before completion and to arrange for you both to sign the document for future reference. This is a pre-printed form largely ignored by the profession to date. It requires little additional work on the part of the solicitor and, of course, you can point to the Law Society good practice guidance as a reason why he should be doing this at no extra cost.

If you can afford it, I strongly recommend that cohabitees contemplating purchasing together spend the extra (maybe £150-200 + VAT) to have a bespoke written Declaration of Trust prepared. This is particularly the case where you intend to make differing contributions to the purchase or the mortgage, or if you plan renovations or a later unequal introduction of capital. A Declaration of Trust can be adapted to take into consideration a variety of circumstances such as anticipated further contributions post-purchase, Right to Buy discounts and offset mortgage facilities.

As with Form 'JO', the benefit of a Declaration of Trust is that it will require the conveyancing solicitor to take explicit instructions from the parties and record the advice given to them about the options available. The Declaration will be professionally prepared, signed by both parties and witnessed. Importantly, it also shows that the parties turned their minds specifically to the question of their shares in the property and went to the trouble of having an agreement prepared for them. In a case where the agreement appears to be unfair to one party, it is important that they each seek or are given the opportunity to obtain independent advice.

NOTES

[16] *Goodman* v. *Gallant* [1985] EWCA Civ 15.

[17] **https://lawsociety.org.uk/support-services/advice/practice-notes/joint-ownership**

[18] Resource 3.

[19] Example at Resource 5.

◆5◆

Financial Help from Relatives

> The Bank of Mum and Dad has... a fantastic reputation as a lender. Long borrowing agreements. No interest to pay, flexible repayment schedules that are sympathetic to the financial setbacks and unexpected expenses we all face. Yes, the Bank of Mum and Dad really has much to recommend it.[20]

Today's housing market has driven young people to seek ever more creative solutions to the gap between house prices and earnings/ mortgage capacity. This often results in parents stepping in to plug the gap between the deposit and mortgage their children can raise and the asking price of a suitable home. It is all too easy for parents to get caught up in the excitement of the house hunt and the frequently urgent need to find the additional money to secure the property for their child. Funds are often advanced by parents without sufficient thought as to the question of what will happen if their child's relationship fails and the house has to be sold or the partner's interest purchased. A 'handshake' or 'gentleman's agreement' is not really good enough in these situations, but it is often all that happens. Sometimes there is no agreement at all about the parents' money. Sometimes there is an agreement for it to be repaid, but nothing is paid. In rare cases, the agreement is documented and repayments are formally recorded.

Many parents and grandparents are advised to gift their hard-earned money to their young relatives as a means of avoiding or reducing inheritance tax on death, making this a very common practice. How would they react if asked to envisage the possibility of their child/grandchild's relationship failing? Would they still gift the money to both parties or just to one? Would they prefer their young relative to enter into an agreement with his or her partner that defines the contribution as his/hers in the event of a separation? Alternatively, would they expect to be repaid? If so, this would no longer constitute a potentially exempt transfer for Inheritance Tax planning purposes.

In the event of a separation where no precautions have been taken, the question inevitably arises: 'how do we deal with Mum and Dad's money?' Opinions will differ, especially further down the line when the partner whose parents did not step in to help has been contributing to the mortgage or paying for improvements, or if there are children of the relationship. From a legal perspective, the question arises whether the funds advanced by the parents were:

a. a loan and, if so, on what terms (i.e. repayable when, and with or without interest); or
b. a gift and, if so, to whom (i.e. to their child or to both parties)?

Situations vary between parents who would want the funds back (or at least to be credited to their child if they knew or suspected that the relationship would end) and those who see the couple as benefitting jointly. Most commonly, where the couple have children, parents/grandparents tend to be more amenable to their funds being regarded as a gift or open to sharing as they want to ensure that their grandchildren are properly housed in the event of a separation. However, introduce a new relationship into this situation or difficulties over post-separation contact with grandchildren, and even that situation can change.

If parents want to be protected from the consequences of the breakdown of their child's relationship and want to avoid being drawn into any dispute, I recommend certain simple precautions. The following questions ought to be asked and (honestly) answered.

- Is this a loan or a gift?
- Will the parents/relatives advancing the money need it back (for example, for retirement income purposes) and, if so, when?
- If it is a loan, should it be written up in some form of agreement? (I certainly recommend it is.)

- Are repayments expected by instalments or is the money repayable at some future date and, if so, when?
- Is it to bear interest and, if so, at what rate?
- What are the triggers to repayment (separation, death, arrears of mortgage, neglect/failure to insure the property)?

POSSIBLE SOLUTIONS

Declaration of Trust

It is not necessary to legally own a property to have a share in it, so a Declaration of Trust can be used to protect a deposit advanced by relatives who will not be the legal owners. At its simplest, a Declaration of Trust will entitle parents to the repayment of their deposit in the form of a fixed or percentage share of the equity in the property. This is then registered at the Land Registry to protect the parents' share. By this method there is absolutely no question about intentions and shares in the event of a separation. This does not necessarily require repayments of the money advanced before sale. The funds could be repayable (with or without interest) on sale of the property. However, consideration should also be given to the extent to which such an arrangement meets the inheritance tax planning of the parents/grandparents making the financial provision.

Mortgage

Parents could take a mortgage over the property to the extent of the funds advanced with a contractual arrangement for repayment with or without interest. This option enables parents to protect their position further by the imposition of covenants such as maintaining the property, paying for buildings insurance and preventing subletting.

As with any secured lender, parents with a mortgage over their child's property have the right to seek repossession if the owners fail to observe the terms of the mortgage deed. This may seem draconian, but it is an important means of minimisimg the scope for dispute in the event of the couple separating. If there is a dispute about issues such as the couple's shares in the home or whether it should be sold, the parents (as mortgagees) have a say. This is because the court would have to take into account the interests of any secured creditor when deciding these matters. The parents would be entitled to push for a sale if (for example) they were concerned that they might not be paid.

I have seen this option used by one very prudent parent who wanted to give her son and his pregnant partner the best chance of making a success of their relationship, but feared it may not last and that her son's partner might not behave particularly fairly. She advanced funds that had been intended to fund her own retirement (i.e. she didn't need to dispose of it to avoid inheritance tax) and which she could ill afford to part with. Unfortunately, her suspicions proved to be correct.

By having a mortgage over the property, she was able to ensure that she was treated in the same way as any secured creditor. The debt to her had to be repaid, the house had to be cared for and insured. Her forethought and strong legal position played a major role in ensuring that the areas of dispute over the property between the young couple were kept within reasonable bounds. She was able to reality check the ambitions of each party to stay in the property (they had to be able to afford her mortgage, etc.) and to ensure that her contribution was treated as a formal loan rather than a 'soft' loan.

The 'granny annexe' or parents transferring property to children

Another solution to the problem of funding a young couple's ambition to get on the property ladder is to purchase with parents or for parents to transfer property to their children during their lifetime (possibly as part of inheritance tax planning arrangements).

In the former case, funds are pooled, the parents' property is sold and a communal home purchased with an annexe or plans to create one to accommodate the parents.

In the latter case, property belonging to the parents is transferred to their child and the parents continue to live there with their child (often with the child's partner and their children).

The benefits are clear; everyone will be accommodated. The parents are on hand to care for children while the young couple work. The couple will be able to provide care for the parents into old age and infirmity. Hopefully, the need for nursing care will be avoided and the parents' capital will not have to be spent on nursing home fees and can pass to their family, either outright or through a trust arrangement.

However, once committed to a joint purchase with family and having sunk funds into the project, neither party can easily afford to buy out the other or purchase a home adequate for their needs, even if they are able to retrieve the whole of their original investment. It is perhaps doubly important for the parties to contemplate the possibility of the arrangement failing and to create an 'exit strategy' for all parties.

There are specific rules on the effect of making transfers that may have the effect of depriving the State of your capital when you need nursing care (see Resource 8 on capital rules on contributions to care home fees and lifetime gifts).

Setting up a trust for your family is complex and must be tailored to your specific needs and those of your family. It is beyond the scope of this work and requires specialist legal advice.

NOTE

[20] The *Guardian* 17 April 2015.

◆6◆

Declaration of Trust and Cohabitation Agreements

A Declaration of Trust can be adapted to a number of different scenarios. It might, for example, treat the deposit paid by one party as a percentage of the total value, which means that the value represented by the deposit will go up or down according to the market value of the home (as will the balance of the value acquired by paying off mortgage borrowing). This means that the shares will always be proportionate to the actual market value of the home.

If the deposit is expressed as a percentage of the gross market value of the home (i.e. ignoring the mortgage), then the person contributing the deposit gets paid on sale and both parties are given equal credit for any mortgage paid between purchase and sale.

In the example below the deposit, provided by Jenny, is £40,000 and the mortgage is £60,000. John, her partner, provides nothing for the deposit, but they contribute equally to the mortgage payments. The value of the house at purchase will look like Figure 1.

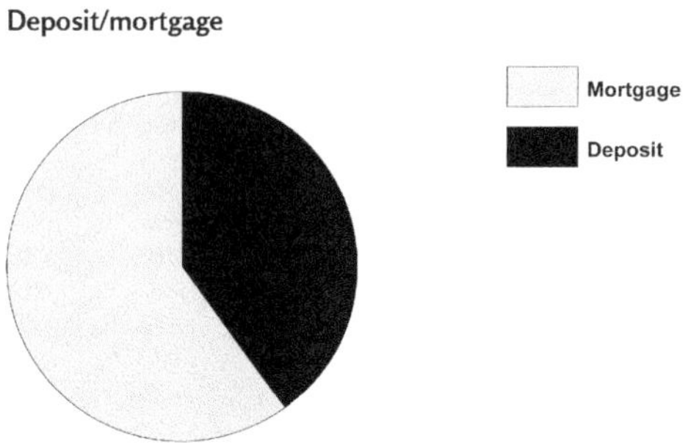

FIGURE 1

After ten years the mortgage has been reduced from £60,000 to £40,000. For the purposes of this illustration, the value is unchanged at £100,000. See Figure 2.

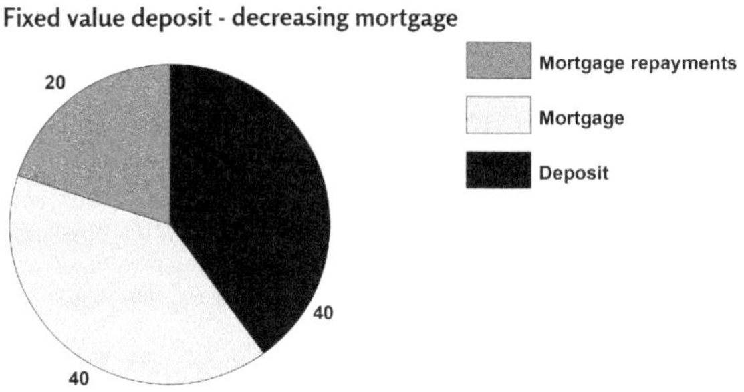

FIGURE 2

The question arises as to how to share the gain in equity of £20,000 (mortgage repayments). A solution would be to share it equally as in Figure 3.

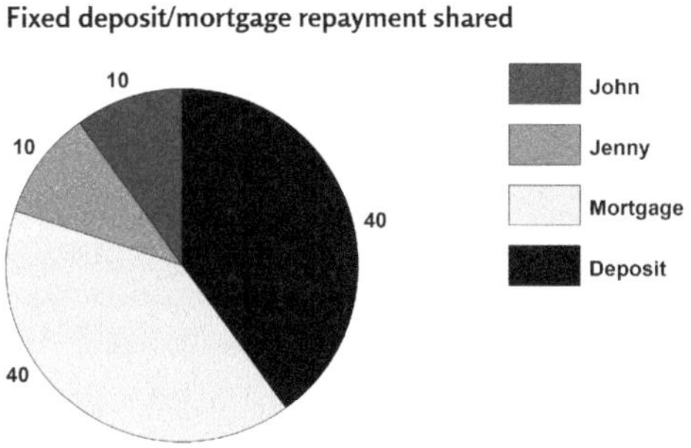

FIGURE 3

On sale, Jenny now recovers her deposit and gains a further £10,000, while John receives £10,000.

SO WHAT HAPPENS WHEN THE MARKET MISBEHAVES AND THE VALUE OF THE HOUSE DECREASES?

Let's assume that the value decreases by £16,000 over the same ten-year period. Assuming Jenny is to recover her deposit as a fixed figure and share any reduction in mortgage borrowing equally with John, the position will now look like Figure 4.

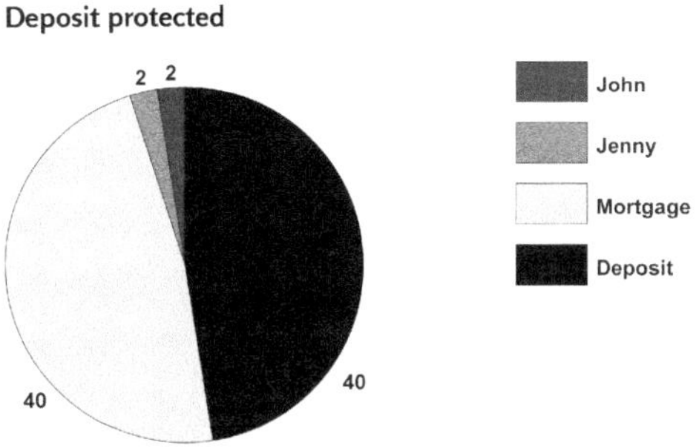

FIGURE 4

In this scenario, John may feel a little aggrieved that his efforts to repay the mortgage have only produced for him equity of £2,000, while Jenny has retained her deposit in full plus gained a further £2,000 through mortgage payments.

An alternative might be to set the losses proportionately against both the deposit contributed by Jenny and the gains made by the jointly paid mortgage. The situation would then look like Figure 5.

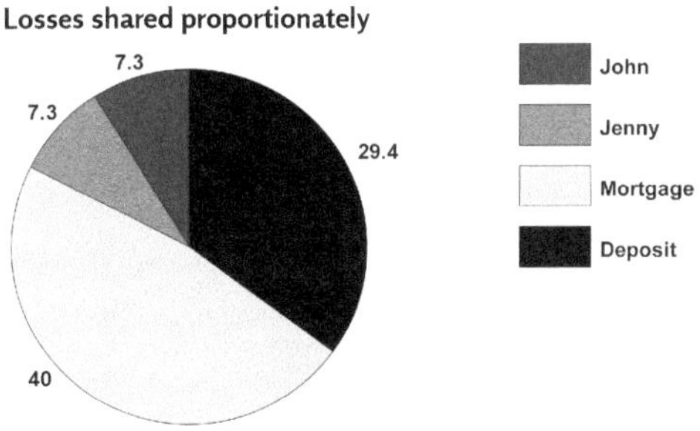

FIGURE 5

In comparison with the example above, each party's share of the equity created by mortgage payments is increased but, overall, Jenny's share is reduced because her deposit is unprotected from the reduction in value. Perhaps it's time for Jenny to feel aggrieved?

LET'S ASSUME THE MARKET IS KIND TO THEM

Let's now assume house prices increase and they make £50,000 in addition to reducing the mortgage by £20,000. Applying the first example, where Jenny's deposit is protected but unchanging, the situation would be as in Figure 6.

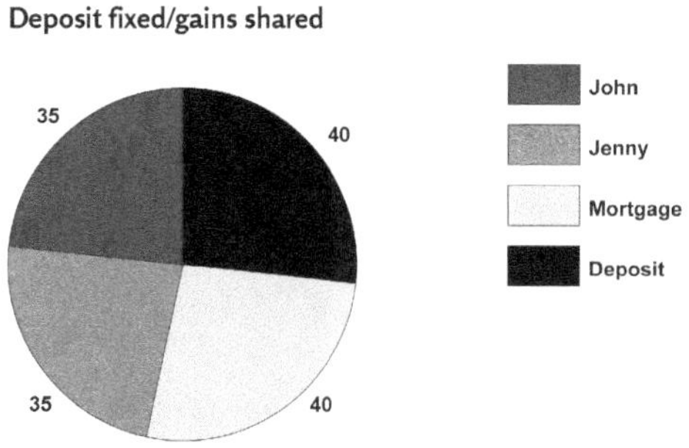

FIGURE 6

Jenny gets her deposit back without any uplift and shares all the uplift and mortgage reduction equally with John. This is the most common arrangement between unmarried couples entering into a Declaration of Trust, but some might say it fails to recognise the risk taken by the party contributing the initial deposit.

To address this, the following arrangement (Figure 7), more in keeping with a commercial arrangement, could be considered. This takes the initial deposit and applies an uplift proportionate to the gain in value of the property.

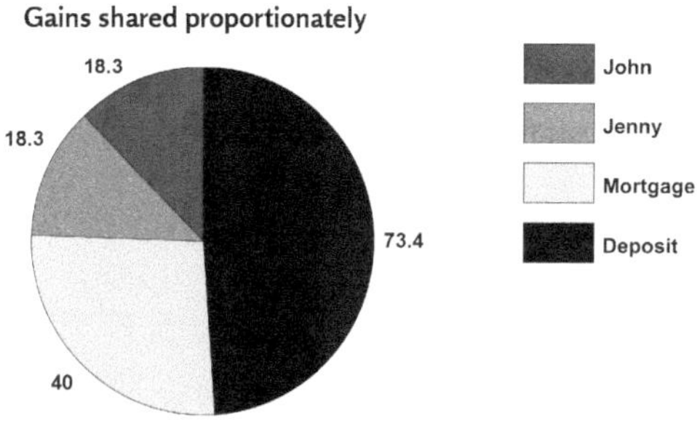

FIGURE 7

So it will be seen that Jenny has benefitted proportionately from the gain in value whereas, if her original deposit had been fixed at £40,000, the position would have been quite different.

OTHER POSSIBLE ARRANGEMENTS

Proportions can be adjusted to take into account differing contributions to the mortgage or other outgoings. A Declaration can also anticipate differing contributions that will be made by one or both partners in the future and provide for a variation in shares that is conditional on the anticipated contribution actually being made.

Agreements that contemplate most of the above situations need to be recorded on purchase in a formal bespoke document rather than the transfer document (TR1) because the latter is not sufficiently flexible or detailed to take into account such matters as differing mortgage contributions. Whatever you decide, provided the Declaration is properly drafted, without pressure on either party and you each receive or acknowledge in writing that you have had the chance to take independent advice, the terms of the Declaration will be conclusive. Remember also that a standard Declaration usually contains a clause to the effect that any change in its terms will only be effective if contained in another similar deed signed by both parties. Therefore, if you choose to go down this route, keep the arrangement under review because, unless and until you agree to change it, it will be binding on you both.

COHABITATION AGREEMENTS

Where a Declaration of Trust deals with 'real property' (land), a Cohabitation Agreement is a statement of the financial arrangements generally between an unmarried cohabiting couple, including arrangements on and after separation, and it can also include a declaration of the parties' interests in shared property. The benefit of Cohabitation Agreements is that, unlike Pre-Nuptial Agreements between married couples, they are not subject to review by a court on separation, save in the limited circumstances described in Chapter 7 below.

One of the commonly expressed fears of people who are reluctant to commit to marriage is the handing over to the courts of ultimate control of financial arrangements in the event of separation. To date, the courts continue to jealously guard their powers to determine financial arrangements on divorce, so that a couple who have tried to pre-determine the arrangements with a Pre-Nuptial Agreement will find that if one of them backs away from it later, the courts can choose those parts of the agreement they do and do not like (although this is now changing - see Chapter 14). There are no such issues for cohabitees. They have absolute freedom to contract with one another and to bind one another to financial arrangements (subject to certain provisions regarding children - see Chapter 17). Cohabitation Agreements can be written in very simple terms or can comprehensively deal with all aspects of the financial arrangements including:

- ownership of personal property (moveable property);
- ownership of gifts;
- maintaining bank accounts (joint or sole);
- responsibility for credit agreements;
- ownership of vehicles;
- responsibility for debts;
- taking and maintaining life insurance cover;
- nomination of pension rights;
- responsibility for living expenses;
- preparation of wills; and
- ownership of inheritances.

There have been attempts to modify such agreements to cover other aspects of couples' relationships. Agreements of the *Fifty Shades of Grey* 'master and servant' variety, which represent an attempt to obligate one party (the servant) to live with the other (among other things), are void on grounds of public policy. The more intimate aspects of a relationship are best left to the couple to decide for themselves, but there is no reason, in principle, why a Cohabitation Agreement should not state in general terms what each party expects of the other, provided there is no element of compulsion or penalty, because such arrangements are not enforceable as a matter of law.

◆7◆

Avoiding Potential Problems with Declarations of Trust or Cohabitation Agreements

ALWAYS FINISH THE JOB

It seems blindingly obvious, but the Declaration of Trust should be signed before completion of the purchase or transfer. It is surprising how often the subject is raised and then shelved. I have seen instances where people took the admirable precaution of instructing their solicitors to prepare Declarations of Trust, only for the solicitors to complete the purchase before the Declaration had been agreed and signed. The incentive for one party to agree the Declaration is then lost or reduced. The solicitor (having caused the problem) will only spend so long chasing before closing the file. The couple are concerned with setting up home and there is a tendency to forget about the Declaration… until separation.

The reason why this is deserving of mention is that on separation the situation is even more confused than if there were no agreement at all. When the solicitor's conveyancing files are disclosed containing unsigned Declarations of Trust, this causes more dispute about what was intended than if there had been no Declaration at all. The moral therefore is: finalise the Declaration before completion of any purchase and if you begin the process of preparing a Declaration of Trust make sure you finish it. Don't rely on the solicitor not to leave loose ends. Ultimately, the responsibility to give instructions rests with you, the client.

Where a properly prepared and executed Declaration of Trust exists, there is very little scope for dispute. That does not mean that when the opportunity presents itself, an aggrieved party won't try to escape from the terms of an agreement they now regret. The only option available to a party who is unhappy with a Declaration of Trust on separation is to try to convince a court to set aside the agreement on the grounds of fraud or mistake. This is a very difficult thing to do, but there are circumstances where the way in which a Declaration of Trust is prepared provides an opportunity to try.

FRAUD AND UNDUE INFLUENCE

Definition of fraud

> Wrongful or criminal deception intended to result in financial or personal gain [21]

Put simply, fraud is commonly understood as dishonesty calculated for personal advantage. Fraud must be proved by showing that the defendant's actions involved five separate elements:

1. a false statement of a material fact;
2. knowledge on the part of the perpetrator that the statement is untrue;
3. intent on the part of the perpetrator to deceive the victim;
4. justifiable reliance by the victim on the statement; and
5. (financial) injury to the victim as a result.

As can be seen from the above list, it is difficult to prove all elements of a fraud. However, ensuring that you both take independent legal advice will overcome any such risks.

More commonly, one party may attempt to rely on a species of fraud known as 'undue influence'.

Definition of undue influence

Influence by which a person is induced to act otherwise than by their own free will or without adequate attention to the consequences.

There are two categories to consider:

1. presumed undue influence; and
2. actual undue influence.

Presumed undue influence

Presumed undue influence arises if the relationship between the parties falls into a class of relationships where, as a matter of law, one party has acquired a position of ascendancy over the other. Such classes include:

- parent/child;
- solicitor/client;
- doctor/patient;
- spouse/spouse.

As can be seen, these are relationships where one party (I will call them 'the persuader') is in a position of trust in relation to the other ('the victim') and could (if they wanted to) influence the victim's decisions in a way that is favourable to the persuader and detrimental to the victim (Doctor: 'Yes I know you're grateful for my medical treatment. Have you considered leaving me a little something in your will? No, there's no need to speak to your relatives or solicitor. I can arrange everything'). In such cases, the burden rests with the persuader as the party benefitting from the agreement to the victim's detriment to prove that they did not abuse the position of trust they occupy with the victim.

Actual undue influence

This covers relationships that do not automatically give rise to a presumption of undue influence but where there is, nonetheless, a relationship between the parties that leads to undue influence. The test is whether one party is already in or assumes a position of ascendancy or influence over the other, or where one party has a dependence on or trust in the other. Many unmarried couples fit this description. If this relationship of ascendancy can be shown to exist by the 'victim' a presumption of undue influence will arise, which means the burden of proving otherwise transfers to the 'persuader', who must now show that, despite the relationship of confidence between them, the 'victim' was still able to exercise their own free will (i.e. that they were not in fact a 'victim' at all).

If undue influence is proved, the agreement is voidable by the innocent party, and the remedy is that the agreement will be rescinded. This means that things will proceed as if the agreement had never been entered into.

Most undue influence cases involve some or all of the following:

- a lack of independent advice to the party who is at a disadvantage;
- an agreement that, to the objective outside observer, appears one-sided;
- some inequality between the parties in terms of age/mental capacity/health/knowledge;
- concealment of facts such as serious debt, a relationship with someone else or plans to end the relationship;
- one party agreeing to take on debt accumulated by the other whether secured against property or unsecured.

A difficult issue that cannot be avoided here is the possibility that the subject of a Declaration of Trust or a Cohabitation Agreement is being raised by a partner who is thinking about separation. I recently came across a Cohabitation Agreement that was followed two weeks after signature by an announcement by one partner of her intention to separate. What she was actually doing was negotiating a Separation Agreement while trying to maintain her partner's goodwill in the knowledge that he would be less helpful if he was told of her true intentions. Fortunately the agreement was relatively fair and not worth challenging. Had it been unfair, she could have faced a claim of undue influence. This is a difficult and very personal subject requiring careful consideration. If the issue of an agreement is raised against the backdrop of difficulties in the relationship, always remember that it is ultimately about what you will each end up with on separation.

If the warning signs are present or there are any doubts as to whether the proposed agreement is fair or may be questioned at a later stage, it is vital that the parties each seek independent advice and reveal all relevant circumstances to those advising them.

OTHER COMMON PROBLEMS WITH DECLARATIONS OF TRUST

A frequent source of dispute between joint purchasers is the Local Authority discount for which one party qualifies when purchasing a council home under the 'Right to Buy' scheme. The discount arises from the combined period of Local Authority tenancy of (usually) one party and can be quite substantial. It is often disregarded in terms of value but, once the clawback period has expired, it immediately creates equity in the property from which any joint owner has benefitted. It has featured as an element in many court actions including the case of *Goodman* v. *Gallant* referred to elsewhere in this book. It is a quantifiable sum (just look at the Local Authority valuation and discount calculation) and should therefore be treated in exactly the same way as a cash deposit.

Another point often missed when making an agreement is the popular 'offset mortgage account' of the kind offered by, for example, the Woolwich, First Direct and Yorkshire Building Society. This clever facility permits borrowers to treat their mortgage much like a current account. Effectively, the owners are borrowing (up to an agreed maximum facility) against their equity when they need it and paying money back in as savings when they don't. The interest earned on the funds in the offset account is set against the mortgage interest. A marvellous idea – until it comes to deciding shares in the property. One then has to carry out a detailed analysis of the offset account transactions to decide who is responsible for any deficit or entitled to credit for any reduction in the mortgage balance. Always ensure you allow for drawings/deposits on the offset account (if there is one) if you are agreeing your shares in your property with your partner.

NOTES

[21] *Oxford English Dictionary* definition.
[22] *OED* definition.
[23] **https://www.gov.uk/right-to-buy-buying-your-council-home/overview**
[24] Usually three years within which the discount is repayable if the home is sold.
[25] **https://www.gov.uk/right-to-buy-buying-your-council-home/selling-your-home**

◆8◆

Banking and Debts

SEPARATE ACCOUNTS

If you and your unmarried partner have separate bank accounts, neither of you can have access to money held in the other's account. If one of you dies, any funds in a sole account will become part of the estate and cannot be used until the estate is settled. On Intestacy (where there is no will) a surviving unmarried partner will have no right to inherit the funds. Liability for any debt or outstanding loans rests solely with the person named on the account.

JOINT ACCOUNTS

If you have a joint account, you both have the right to access the money in the account (unless one or both of you give instructions to your bank to ensure that withdrawals require joint signatures). Even though you are unmarried, if one of you should die the whole account would immediately become the property of the other. To close a joint account, banks require the consent of both parties. If the account is not officially closed by both parties this could mean that one of you could run up an overdraft and leave the other responsible for it. If trust is lost, the bank will usually accept instructions from one party to freeze an account or require joint signatures for any withdrawals.

CREDIT CARD OR PERSONAL LOAN

You are liable if a credit card is in your name, even if your partner is a 'named user'. If the card is held jointly, then you are both liable. If there is any sign of money worries or a tendency to run up debt, this requires early consideration. Ask yourself, should you be holding named user credit cards?

If you take out a loan agreement with your partner, you are both responsible for repaying the borrowed amount.

DEBTS

Regardless of whether you marry your partner or not, you are inevitably subject to one another's fortunes in many ways over time. For example, if one of you is unable to pay his or her share of a joint mortgage or rent, then that responsibility falls to the other (until such time as matters are resolved by agreement, separation or court order). However, unmarried partners are not responsible for the debts incurred by the other in his/her separate name.

Unfortunately, over time, unresolved debt problems for one partner can have an adverse effect on the position of the other, as many people affected by this will testify. The indebted partner cannot afford to contribute to the outgoings. The other ends up paying far more with little hope of recovering the money. If one party is forced to pay the mortgage and maintain the jointly owned home without help from the other for a long time they might want the equity to be divided unequally on sale of the property. This may be possible but would depend on there being no agreement about shares (see Chapter 6) or convincing a court to conduct an 'equitable account'. Where the property has been re-mortgaged or charged post-purchase by both owners, but for the exclusive benefit of one of them, then it may also be possible to persuade the court to conduct an 'equitable account' between the parties on separation so that the shares would be divided in a way that recognises this benefit to one owner. This option would be available even where there is a binding agreement about shares on purchase.

It is important to remember that the legal cost of pursuing such claims may outweigh the benefit. A detailed examination of contributions and benefit (bank statements, etc.) will be required. There is rarely clarity about who benefitted ('OK, so I spent the re-mortgage money on the pickup truck but I used it to earn money in my business for both of us!'). The partner with debt may be sued by creditors. This can lead to court judgements for money, which in turn leads to attempts by creditors to enforce the debt that can affect the solvent partner in various ways. A judgement creditor may attempt enforcement by various methods:

1. Charging Order

An application for a charge (similar to a mortgage) to be placed over the debtor's interest in any property he owns (for example, the family home). This won't affect the other partner's share (if they are joint owners), but the creditor may later apply for an order for its sale if the charge is for a significant sum. A joint owner would receive notice of any such application and would be entitled to make representations at court.

2. Bailiff's warrant

The court bailiff will visit the home seeking moveable assets of value belonging to the debtor. Joint assets or things belonging to the solvent partner are sometimes seized. The solvent partner will have to produce evidence of purchase or ownership to the local court or Sheriff's Officer to get them back. Joint assets can be sold by a bailiff in possession and the dispute passes to the proceeds of sale of the item concerned. There are detailed rules about what the bailiff can and cannot take and the circumstances in which they are entitled to force entry to your home[26].

3. Attachment of Earnings

A court order is made for the debtor's salary to be deducted at source to satisfy the debt by instalments. He will have 'protected earnings' still but inevitably less money to contribute to household outgoings.

4. Third Party Debt Order (TPDO)

A court order is made that freezes a debtor's bank account to the extent of the judgement debt owed (provided there is a credit balance), or against any money held by a third person or organisation on behalf of the debtor (for example, a conveyancing solicitor on the sale of a property). The initial order is made without notice to the debtor so that they don't have a chance to move the money. The court then decides at a 'return hearing' to whom the money belongs[27]. The net result is potential hardship for the solvent partner who has to take the financial reins.

5. Statutory Demand/Creditor's Bankruptcy Petition

As an alternative to Court enforcement procedures, a creditor who is owed at least £750 by either an individual or a company can issue a statutory demand. This is a relatively simple low cost procedure. If the individual or company does not properly deal with the demand within 21 days this is grounds for the creditor to request the Court to issue either a winding-up petition (in the case of a company) or a bankruptcy petition (in the case of an individual, provided the amount due is at least £5,000).

PROTECTIVE MEASURES

Instead of waiting for a creditor taking action to recover a debt, a debtor who is insolvent (i.e. having more liabilities than assets or not being able to pay liabilities when they fall due) can improve their position by various methods.

1. Debt Relief Order (DRO)

These are for people on low incomes who are not able to pay their debts. The cost is £90 and in order to be eligible you must owe less than £20,000; you cannot own assets worth more than £1,000; you cannot own a car that is worth more than £1,000; and, after paying all your usual household bills, you must not have more than £50 left over each month. If your DRO application is accepted, all your debts are written off after 12 months.

2. Individual Voluntary Arrangement (IVA)

A very viable alternative to bankruptcy for many people, especially when they either have assets they want try to keep or where bankruptcy would mean that they may, for example, lose their job. The IVA proposal (which is either accepted or rejected by the debtor's creditors) is essentially a contract between the debtor and his creditors whereby, in return for the creditors not making him bankrupt, the debtor offers to pay a dividend to creditors over a period of time. In practice this dividend will be greater than creditors would have received in the event of the debtor's bankruptcy.

Usually, the proposal will either provide for an immediate payment to creditors (usually from a third party such as a relative) in full and final settlement of his debts or the debtor will agree to pay a monthly amount to the Supervisor of his IVA (an independent insolvency practitioner (IP)) over a period of time. The Supervisor then pays these monies to the creditors, again in full and final settlement of the debts. The length of time that an IVA can last for varies considerably but usually it is for a period (often around five years) that is sufficient to pay creditors a reasonable dividend, often of around 50 per cent of their debts. The balance due to creditors is written off at the end of a successful IVA.

In order to enter into an IVA, a debtor would normally consult with an IP to draw up the proposal, which is then put to the creditors at a meeting. The cost of drawing up this proposal and calling the meeting of creditors is usually between £2,500 and £5,000. Once agreed, the cost of supervising the IVA is paid out of the contributions received from the debtor before they are paid to creditors.

Points a debtor should bear in mind when considering whether or not an IVA is suitable will include the following:

1. Details of all IVAs are entered onto an Individual Insolvency Register operated by the Insolvency Service. Your credit rating is likely to be affected.
2. If you are unable to maintain the monthly payments, or make good any shortfall within a short time, it is likely that the Supervisor of the IVA will be required to make you bankrupt.
3. Your income and expenditure will be monitored closely and the proposal will probably provide for monthly contributions to increase if your earnings go up.
4. If the main reason that you entered into an IVA is to save a jointly or solely owned property, it is likely that one of the requirements will be that the property should be revalued towards the end of the IVA and any equity introduced into the IVA (by, for example, re-mortgage).

3. Bankruptcy

Although making a debtor bankrupt is an option available to a creditor, a debtor also has the option to make himself bankrupt. The application form (available on the Insolvency Service's website[28]) is taken to the local Court. The fee and receiver's deposit is £705 (as at April 2015). The debtor is made bankrupt either immediately or as soon as an appropriate appointment can be made before the judge.

The Official Receiver (an official in the Insolvency Service) is then immediately appointed as Trustee in Bankruptcy but, if there are assets worth recovering, this role is often transferred to an independent Insolvency Practitioner whose job it is to investigate the conduct of the bankrupt in the period prior to the bankruptcy and to gather in his assets to distribute proportionately between the creditors. Certain assets are exempt from this process including most pensions, tools of the trade and normal domestic furniture and equipment (often including a motor vehicle).

It is important to note that, once a bankruptcy order is made against an individual, all his assets (except any exempt assets) are automatically transferred to (or vested in) his Trustee. The only person who can sell a debtor's interest in a property will be his Trustee in Bankruptcy.

In normal circumstances, the duration of a bankruptcy is one year and a debtor will get his discharge automatically at the end of this time. The effect of this is that the bankrupt will be freed from most of his debts. There are some exceptions which include fines, debts arising from fraud and certain debts arising from family proceedings such as maintenance.

It is very important to note, however, that assets which passed to the Trustee at the beginning of the bankruptcy do not pass back to the debtor after the discharge has been achieved. For example, where the debtor's interest in a property, such as a jointly owned property for example, passed to his Trustee, the Trustee remains the only person who can deal with that interest in the property even after the bankrupt has received his discharge. A more detailed discussion of jointly owned property can be found below.

The main effects of bankruptcy are as follows:

- You are not allowed to carry on a business in a name other than that in which you were made bankrupt without telling your creditors.
- You cannot take part in running or managing a company without the agreement of the Court, either as a director or not.
- You cannot incur credit of more than £500 without telling the provider of that credit that you are bankrupt.
- You cannot hold certain public offices.
- You can have a bank account and many banks now operate basic bank accounts that are suitable for bankrupts.
- Your income and necessary expenditure will be assessed by the Trustee and any 'surplus' income may be taken by the Trustee for a period of up to three years (an Income Payments Order).

- As with an IVA, a bankruptcy is noted on the Individual Insolvency Register. Once a bankrupt has received his discharge the credit status is likely to be affected for a period of up to five years.

In the period leading up to bankruptcy there are various 'offences' that can be committed by a debtor, sometimes in innocence. An insolvent joint owner will sometimes transfer their share of property to their partner, but the transaction can later be challenged by a trustee in bankruptcy[29]. There are two different forms of avoidance.

1. Transactions at undervalue

If, in the five years before going bankrupt, a debtor gives away an asset (including to an unmarried partner) either for no value or for less than it is actually worth, a Trustee can challenge the transaction and, in effect, reverse the transaction in order to obtain the proper value for the benefit of creditors. For example if, shortly before going bankrupt, a debtor tries to transfer his interest in a jointly owned property to his partner for no money, a Court can reverse the transaction.

2. Voidable preferences

If, within six months of the bankruptcy (or two years if it is to someone who is 'connected' to the debtor), the debtor does something that puts a creditor in a better position than he would have been if it didn't happen, then the Court can restore the position to what it would have been. For example, if, before declaring himself bankrupt, a debtor sells his car and uses the money to repay a loan to his partner so that, after bankruptcy, the partner is owed nothing whereas other creditors are owed the full amount of their debts, the partner can be forced to repay the money if the car sale and payment to the partner took place within two years before the bankruptcy (because the partner is connected to the debtor).

When deciding between the various options open to someone who is insolvent, it is very important to obtain proper, independent advice and to carefully consider all the options. People often think that an IVA is best because they think it is less onerous than bankruptcy. In fact, in many simple cases, bankruptcy should be the preferred option for the following reasons.

- It only lasts for one year compared with usually around five years for an IVA.

- An IVA usually presupposes that you are going to make a monthly contribution for the benefit of your creditors. In bankruptcy, and particularly where there are dependants, quite large amounts can be earned before an Income Payments Order is sought by the Trustee.
- You can be close to the conclusion of an IVA when unforeseen circumstances could mean that the IVA fails with the result that bankruptcy follows.
- Even if a property is owned, in many cases this can still be retained in bankruptcy (see below).

Jointly owned property

The main impact of many bankruptcies relates to the home, which is often the only asset for the creditors. It is often jointly owned with the debtor's partner. The interest of any Trustee will be limited to the debtor's share of any equity that may be available in the property, after taking into account any mortgage on the property and also any other charges that may have been registered against it. In most cases, notwithstanding the bankruptcy of one or both of the owners of a property and provided the mortgage continues to be paid, the Trustee will allow the family to stay in the property for at least a period of time.

Where there is no equity in the property, the Official Receiver, or any Trustee appointed, will usually allow the non-bankrupt partner to acquire the bankrupt's interest in the property for £1 plus a small contribution towards legal costs.

The situation where there is equity in the property is slightly more complicated. The general rule is that, for the first 12 months, the interests of the bankrupt's dependants will take priority and a Trustee will not do anything to remove them from the property. But, after a year, the interests of the debtor's creditors come first and a Trustee may try to sell the property to raise money to pay the creditors. Prior to this the Trustee will need to obtain an order for the possession of the property from the Court and, in most cases, it will be granted.

It is important to realise though that the sole objective of a Trustee is to realise the bankrupt's share of the property. He has to wait for at least a year and will incur a lot of legal and other costs to obtain possession of it and then to sell it. This provides an opportunity for the non-bankrupt partner to acquire the bankrupt's interest in the property from the Trustee for less than it is actually worth.

The first step is to get a good idea of the equity in the property. You can get a good idea from local knowledge and the Land Registry property price records[30] or by obtaining a valuation from a local agent. It is important to note that in these negotiations the Trustee is also likely to want his own independent advice. The ideal situation is where the non-bankrupt partner has access to funds from, for example, a relative, which enables them to make an offer to the Trustee for the bankrupt's share of the equity early in the bankruptcy. If the Trustee does not have to wait a year to sell the property and then does not have to go through the sales process, the savings in costs can be considerable and most Trustees will be willing to give a significant discount on the value of the equity to take account of these savings.

There will be situations though where, because of the breakdown of the relationship, the non-bankrupt partner does not want to remain in the jointly owned property. In these cases, provided the mortgage continues to be paid, there will be no pressure on the non-bankrupt partner and any children to leave the property for the first 12 months. Once they have left the property and it becomes vacant, the Trustee will be able to sell the property (and is under a duty to get the best possible price). The appropriate share of any equity will then be available to the non-bankrupt partner in due course. Very often it will be in the interests of the non-bankrupt partner to remain in the property while it is being sold in order to maximise the sale price. This should be discussed with the Trustee at the time.

Where the property is owned by your bankrupt partner and you have no legal interest in it but think you might have a financial interest in it (see Chapter 16), it is still possible to make a claim, but the situation is more complex and you will need urgent specialist legal advice to protect your position.

You can expect credit reference problems by association with an insolvent or bankrupt partner because credit reference agencies record details not only against his name but also the address. This means you may struggle to secure credit unless you can convince the credit reference agencies to change or note their records to draw a distinction between you and your partner for the purposes of any adverse credit reference checks. You can carry out a credit check online for a small fee[31]. You will need your partner's consent to carry out a credit check for him/her.

Therefore, you can see that bankruptcy carries with it potentially serious risks for the solvent as well as the insolvent party. Some people try to overcome this by asking the transferring partner to complete a 'Declaration of Solvency' (a statement of their financial affairs at the time of the transfer) to demonstrate that when the property was transferred or given away, they were still able to manage their debts. This does not render the transaction totally safe from the attentions of a trustee in bankruptcy, but may help to protect the person to whom the asset was transferred.

NOTES

[26] https://www.citizensadvice.org.uk/debt-and-money/action-your-creditor-can-take/bailiffs/letting-a-bailiff-into-your-home/can-a-bailiff-force-entry-into-your-home/

[27] https://www.citizensadvice.org.uk/debt-and-money/action-your-creditor-can-take/creditor-takes-money-from-your-bank-account/

[28] https://www.gov.uk/government/organisations/insolvency-service

[29] Insolvency Act 1986 ss.339 and 341 refers.

[30] http://houseprices.landregistry.gov.uk/

[31] http://www.experian.co.uk/creditexpert2/04_credit_score.html?sc=701371&gclid=CIbi68_i8oCFcWVGwod7wKlg

◆9◆

Income and Taxation

If you and your partner live together as a couple, but are not married, you are treated as two separate individuals. This makes a difference to how you are taxed. Married couples and civil partners have certain advantages because they are given tax exemptions for Capital Gains Tax and Inheritance Tax. In the following chapters all references to spouses and married couples shall include civil partners.

PROPERTY TAXATION

The main home

A valuable relief from capital gains tax is available on what is known in tax terms as the 'principal private residence' (PPR). The statutory definition of PPR is that no part of a gain on a private residence is chargeable to capital gains tax (CGT) if:

1. The property is the individual's main or only residence throughout the entire period of ownership; and
2. The residence has only been used as a home and nothing else.

There are other points to note for PPR relief to be available in full but these are outside the scope of this text. Principal Private Residence relief is a complicated area and professional advice should be sought including where the statutory definition is met but the garden is more than 0.5 hectares.

A married couple living together are only eligible to claim PPR relief on one property between them. Where they own a second property and both properties are used by them as a residence it is possible to make an election, within two years of acquiring the second property, as to which is to be their PPR.

Each time an additional property is acquired a new election must be made.

Where a couple are living together but are not married it is possible, given the right circumstances, that each of them can own a property that is eligible to be their PPR. First of all, for PPR relief to be available, the properties must both be in use as a residence for the owners. For example:

> Brian and Mandy live together and are working in London. Brian owns a property in London where they live Monday to Thursday. On Friday they travel down to Cornwall where they spend the weekend in Mandy's Cornish property.
>
> When they started living together, although neither of them own two properties, they nevertheless have a second property available for their use. They were both advised by their accountant to make a tax election within the first two years of availability as to which property is to be treated as their PPR. Brian elected for the London property to be treated as his PPR, Mandy elected for the property in Cornwall to be treated as her PPR.

If you are in a similar position to Brian and Mandy but have not made the election within the first two years all is not lost. HMRC have authority to extend the period in certain circumstances and if you have failed to make the election within the two years because you were unaware of the election it may be possible to arrange for an extension to the time limit under ESC D21. An alternate strategy is if one of the properties were to be sold and a new one purchased this will reopen the two-year time limit for electing which property is to be each person's PPR. In addition, if Brian and Mandy were to become married, this would start a new period where only one election of a PPR could be made going forward.

In the event of two properties being available and no election in place the decision on which property is the PPR will be made on a matter of fact. HMRC will look for quality of occupation over quantity and will consider matters such as third party post, where you are registered to vote and where your place of work is. So beware, not making an election does not make full use of tax exemptions available and can lead to an unexpected CGT liability in the future.

For an unmarried couple to take maximum advantage of the relief it is recommended that each own one property wholly rather than both properties being held in joint names. Where both properties are held in joint names careful consideration should be given as to which you want to be the PPR. If Brian elects for the London property to be his PPR and Mandy for the Cornwall property to be her PPR and the London property is sold, only one half of the capital gain will be eligible for the exemption as the gain on Mandy's share is not covered as she elected for the Cornwall property to be her PPR.

One property with a large gain may point the way as to which to make the election for; a short ownership period for one property and a long intended period for the other may be another factor. Once an election is in place it is possible to make further elections to vary which property is to be treated as the PPR. There are other issues relating to PPR that are outside the scope of this publication and, as ever, the best advice is to consult with a competent tax advisor.

Buy-to-let properties

A popular form of investment for the unmarried is to purchase buy-to-let properties. There are a number of issues to consider when ensuring that the investment is as tax efficient as possible.

At the time of purchase Stamp Duty Land Tax (SDLT) will be paid by the purchaser. Where the purchaser already owns a residential property there will be a three per cent SDLT surcharge over the normal SDLT payable. If the purchase is being made in joint names and either of the joint purchasers already owns a residential property the surcharge will apply. If one partner in an unmarried couple owns a residential property and the other does not the SDLT surcharge will not apply if the buy-to-let property is purchased in the sole name of the partner who does not own a residential property.

A change is being introduced over a transitional period to restrict the relief for interest paid on borrowings for buy-to-let properties. Prior to 6 April 2016 relief was given for interest paid against the rental income received. For a higher rate taxpayer this meant relief was available at 40 per cent and for an additional rate payer relief was available at 45 per cent. Once the transitional period is completed by the tax year 2019/20 relief will be given not as a deduction from income but as a relief from tax payable, with the relief being at basic rate – currently 20 per cent. For 2016/17 75 per cent of the interest will be relieved as a deduction from income and 25 per cent of the interest will attract a tax deduction at basic rate. This will change to 50 per cent:50 per cent for 2017/18 and 25 per cent:75 per cent for 2018/19.

Some buy-to-let owners are looking to incorporate their property letting businesses (to 'go limited') to avoid this restriction on relief. Such a proposal needs to be discussed with your tax advisor to ensure that this is a suitable solution in your circumstances.

The tax rates of the partners may influence how the property should be purchased, irrespective of relief for interest paid on a buy-to-let mortgage. One interesting factor may be that one partner is providing the majority of the funds and wants a greater share of the ownership, but is the partner who is paying the highest rate of income tax. Where a property is owned jointly the income can either be shared in the ratios of ownership or equally. Thus if Mandy provides 90 per cent of the funding and Brian 10 per cent they may wish to own the property in those ratios. However, if Mandy is a higher rate tax payer and Brian a basic rate tax payer it will be more efficient for them to share the income equally for tax purposes.

Married couples do not have the same level of flexibility and will always be treated as receiving income in equal shares, unless they make an election to HMRC to vary the income shares supported by a document varying the legal and equitable interest in the property.

To own property in unequal shares it is necessary to hold it as tenants in common (see Chapter 4). A joint tenancy ownership will always be held in equal shares.

Another important change in income tax for furnished property letting was the removal of a wear and tear allowance with effect from 6 April 2016. This has been changed to a repairs and renewals basis from that date. Wear and tear provided a 10 per cent relief (being 10 per cent of rental income) irrespective of the actual expenditure in the year. Repairs and renewals relief is on actual expenditure when existing items are either repaired or renewed. Care is needed to ensure the repair or renewal is on a like-for-like basis, otherwise part or all of the expenditure may be disallowed as capital expenditure.

Short-term furnished holiday lettings

Where property is let as holiday accommodation rather than for residential lettings there may be some important tax benefits available. This will depend on whether or not the lettings qualify as Short-Term Furnished Holiday Lettings (STFHL). The main conditions are as follows.

1. The property must be furnished to a standard that enables occupation without the provision of furniture by the guests.
2. It must be available to the general public for use as holiday accommodation for at least 210 days in a 12-month period.
3. It must be so let for at least 105 days in the 12-month period.
4. Occupation must not be to the same person for more than 31 days within the 210-day period. This will allow out-of-season lets for up to 155 days as long as the person to whom the out-of-season let is made does not occupy the property within the 210-day period.

The tax benefits of qualifying as STFHL are that the lettings will be treated as a trade for tax purposes. In turn this will mean that the following reliefs will be available.

1. The income generated will qualify as relevant income for pension scheme contributions.
2. In the event of a loss being made the loss will be available for set off against other taxable income rather than being used against only rental income in the same year or future years.
3. When the whole or part of a STFHL business is disposed of any capital gain may be eligible for capital gains tax entrepreneurs' relief, where the tax rate is 10 per cent rather than 18 or 28 per cent depending on the size of the gain and the status of the taxpayer.
4. Subject to reinvestment rules, reinvestment relief will be available or hold over relief in the event of gifting.

OTHER TAXATION ISSUES

Trading as sole trader / in partnership

Where one cohabitant runs a business, employment of the other cohabitant can provide tax relief for the business. Certain issues need to be considered and, in particular, any remuneration should be at a commercial rate. The danger of paying a cohabitant an excessive salary is that, while this will remain taxable income for the cohabitant as an employee, it may be disallowed to the extent it exceeds a commercial level of salary for the business.

Where this is a potential problem consideration can be given to the possibility of bringing the cohabitant in as a business partner. The way in which partnership profits are shared is a matter for agreement between the business partners and this may enable a greater shifting of taxable income from one partner to another. Care does need to be taken to ensure there is a genuine partnership arrangement with partners' meetings, responsibilities for each partner and provision of capital by each partner. A written partnership agreement is highly recommended.

Limited companies

Many businesses trade in corporate form, sometimes for the comfort of limited liability, sometimes for kudos and sometimes for tax efficiency. One cohabitant may be more involved with the business than the other but this does not stop them both being director/shareholders in the company. Care needs to be taken to ensure that any remuneration that is paid is at a commercial level otherwise some of the cost may be disallowed in the corporation tax computation. However, the ability to share income between cohabitants is not restricted to remuneration in a corporate situation as dividends can be paid to shareholders. Where different share classes are used dividends can be very flexible.

The taxation of dividends has changed with effect from 6 April 2016. The previous system of attaching tax credits to dividends that were deemed to satisfy basic rate tax has been abandoned. Each taxpayer now has a dividend allowance of £5,000 each year and no tax is charged on dividends falling within this allowance. For dividends over and above the allowance a basic rate taxpayer is charged tax at 7.5 per cent, a higher rate tax payer 32.5 per cent and an additional rate tax payer 38.1 per cent. This represents an increase of 7.5 per cent across the range of taxpayers in comparison with the previous system, once dividends exceed £5,000. Nevertheless, it does present an opportunity for some tax efficiency between the cohabitants by making full use of the dividend allowances and sharing the dividend income between the cohabitants to make full use of personal allowances and basic rate bands.

Where possible, cohabitants should be involved at the commencement of the company while the share values are at par. Introduction of a partner as a shareholder when the company has been trading for some number of years can present a problem, with the transfer of shares from one cohabitant to another creating a capital gain.

A decision about whether to incorporate a business and, if so, who to appoint as directors or shareholders and what level of remuneration to pay and the dividend policy are complex issues and should be fully discussed with your tax advisors.

Capital Gains Tax

When chargeable assets are disposed of capital gains tax will be an issue. This will apply to assets transferred between cohabitants whether it is by way of sale, gift or exchange of property. For a married couple any sale or transfer of properties between them is made at 'no gain, no loss' for capital gains tax purposes. This is not the case for unmarried couples and this means you should take care when sales or transfers are made between cohabitants.

The previous section has talked about involving cohabitants in an incorporated business and potential difficulties where it is an established business. If shares are gifted from one partner to another it is deemed for tax purposes that they are transferred at open market value. With a successful trade it is quite possible that a value for goodwill has been generated and, although this is not reflected in the balance sheet, it will be taken into account in a valuation for capital gains tax purposes.

There are ways in which a capital gain can be deferred, thus removing the cash flow disadvantage of paying tax on the transfer. Certain assets are eligible to hold over relief where assets are gifted and, most importantly, assets eligible to agricultural property relief or business property relief qualify. For the transfer of shares in a trading company the claiming of hold over relief may be a solution to deferring a capital gain. It is important to note that any held over gain will be brought into charge on a subsequent disposal.

For non-business assets (with some exceptions surrounding properties on which PPR may be claimed in the future) it may be practical to obtain hold over relief through the use of a discretionary trust. This will be a chargeable transfer for inheritance tax purposes but if it is within the available nil rate band of the transferor no IHT charge arises. At a later point the asset can be transferred out of the settlement and any gain held over by the trustees.

The message here is that before transferring assets between cohabitants discuss your proposals with your tax advisor to see what the capital gains tax consequences will be and what steps can be taken to defer the liability.

Inheritance Tax

For a married couple no inheritance tax is charged on inter-spouse transfers, whether they are made during lifetime or following death. There is a standard nil rate band of £325,000 for each taxpayer and any proportion unused on first death can be transferred to the surviving spouse.

Unmarried cohabitants do not benefit from this treatment and transfers between them are chargeable to IHT. There is also no ability to transfer any unused nil rate band between unmarried cohabitants. This does mean that it is even more important for unmarried couples to ensure that their estates are properly planned for succession.

The first advice is to ensure that both cohabitants have a valid will in place. Not only does this ensure that administration of an estate is easier and more cost effective, it also ensures that the estate devolves in the way that you wish. Bear in mind that the intestate rules do not provide for the transfer of assets to the surviving partner in an unmarried couple situation.

Utilisation of nil rate bands will be important to ensure that none are wasted. In the event of a surviving partner needing the ability to have access to income or capital from the deceased cohabitant's estate it is possible to use discretionary nil rate band trusts within the will drafting. The surviving partner can have the security of access by being included as a beneficiary without rolling both estates into one and potentially paying IHT twice on the same assets.

Another point to watch will be taking advantage of the additional nil rate band available where the family home is passed down to the next generation. Once the transitional period for introduction of the relief has been completed by 2019/20 this will increase the nil rate band to £500,000.

For larger estates there is a wide range of IHT planning that can be undertaken in conjunction with your tax advisor, but is too wide a subject to cover here.

◆10◆

Business Interests - A Typical Scenario

We dealt earlier with the opportunities for the unmarried to make the most of their tax advantages in business. However, it often doesn't work out like that. What about those who end up running businesses together with no clear indication of ownership of the business or profit sharing? This can add another dimension to financial disputes on separation, which doesn't exist at all for a divorcing couple in the same situation. For those who are married all assets (including business interests) are in 'the pot' for division between the couple without the need to prove ownership. For the unmarried, ownership is all, so this issue must be addressed as a preliminary point if there is a dispute about ownership.

A well-known and fairly typical recent example is the 2012 case of *Geary* v. *Rankine*[32]. Mr Rankine and Ms Geary were in a relationship between 1990 and 2009. They had one child born in 1992. Mrs Geary had been married but didn't divorce her husband until 2002. In 1996, Mr Rankine purchased a guesthouse for £61,000 mortgage free, using his redundancy package. It was initially intended that the business would be run by a manager but, eventually, Mr Rankine managed it himself and Mrs Geary (no doubt thinking it would benefit them both) gave up her job in London to come and help him.

When they separated, Mrs Geary claimed that:

1. she had acquired a share in the guesthouse itself; and
2. they had been partners in the guesthouse business.

Mrs Geary received no salary and admitted that she felt Mr Rankine was very controlling about how much she spent. Mr Rankine refused to grant Mrs Geary any security by providing for her in his will or making her a partner in the business. He said that he didn't feel he should do so until she had at least divorced her ex-husband. Even when she did, he remained non-committal in response to her requests for security. Only he drew from the business and only he received the profits. The business accounts and bank accounts were in his sole name.

Mrs Geary claimed that she was entitled to a share. She said that although he bought the guesthouse the intention later changed so that they agreed that it was to be 'theirs'. She said that the fact she had given up her London job showed how she had relied on the agreement to her personal detriment (see Chapter 16 – 'Resulting and Constructive Trusts'). She also said that the fact she was heavily involved in the business and received no wage pointed to a partnership. The property itself, she said, was a partnership asset and ought to be shared between them. She said that living together off the profits showed that the business was a partnership.

The court rejected her claims. The fact that the property was purchased as a business investment actually worked against her. Had it been purchased purely as a home for them her task would have been easier but, as will be seen in Chapter 16, the one area where the resulting trust principle is alive and well is in relation to property purchased in the course of a business. Mr Rankine had provided all the money to purchase it so, on a resulting trust basis, all the value in the property would belong to him. On the evidence, the court found that Mr Rankine had never led Mrs Geary to believe that she would have an interest in the property.

In relation to the business it was found that:

1. the business accounts were drawn up with Mr Rankine as a sole trader;
2. he made all the drawings;
3. the business profits were not shared (except in the sense that Mr Rankine permitted them both to live off of them);
4. Mrs Geary was protected from liabilities;
5. Mrs Geary was not described to others (trade creditors, customers, suppliers, etc.) as 'a partner'.

In this case we have a clash of old-fashioned chauvinistic attitudes with the growing acceptance of unmarried cohabitation as a mainstream family model. Mr Rankine apparently felt strongly that Mrs Geary should obtain her divorce but, at the same time, was prepared to form a serious relationship with her, producing a child and he came to depend on her to help run the business. Mrs Geary, having had a child with Mr Rankine, committed herself wholeheartedly to the relationship, giving up her job and working unpaid in the business. Not surprisingly, over time she felt the need for security for herself and (in due course) her child. Mr Rankine, on the other hand, permitted her to do all this, seemingly without anticipating any adverse consequences in terms of her taking that as a sign that she had some entitlement for herself. The failure of her claim is in some ways irrelevant. The case, ending as it did in the Court of Appeal, was catastrophic for them both in terms of the legal costs, time and distress.

Most of us can appreciate where things went wrong with the benefit of hindsight, but let's consider for a moment what they could each have done to avoid dispute. The seeds of this dispute were tied up in a number of different elements that, if broken down and examined individually, could have been addressed to the satisfaction of each of them. We will look at this from the perspective of each partner in turn, examining the mistakes or incorrect assumptions they made about their own or their partner's position.

MRS GEARY

Mrs Geary really should have resolved her outstanding divorce with her former husband. That was clearly a cause of anxiety to Mr Rankine. Once she and Mr Rankine had a child together she no doubt felt vulnerable in the relationship. She did, however, have some leverage, had she used it at the right moment. Before Mrs Geary gave up her job in London and threw herself wholeheartedly into the business, she should have insisted on an understanding of her position in relation to the business. Realistically, she could not at that stage have expected to acquire an actual interest in the property itself, because it was common ground that Mr Rankine had contributed all the purchase money. However, she could have suggested that she might begin to acquire an interest by making contributions to the mortgage and entering into a Declaration of Trust to preserve Mr Rankine's original contribution. Thus protected, Mr Rankine may have been sufficiently reassured to agree.

An interest in the business they were going to work in together (the option of employing a manager having been rejected) in the form of a partnership with Mr Rankine would have given Mrs Geary a measure of security and possibly allayed any concerns Mr Rankine would have had about her intentions in relation to the property. The business partnership agreement could (and should) specify what is (and is not) partnership property, so Mr Rankine could easily have taken the guesthouse freehold out of the equation while offering Mrs Geary some security within the business. An interest in the business would not of itself guarantee anything for Mrs Geary (all business involves risk and this business was no more than a means of earning a living with little or no intrinsic value), but she clearly wanted to feel involved and appreciated for all that she did for their joint benefit and to have a chance to share in the fruits of that.

MR RANKINE

For his part, Mr Rankine should not have assumed that Mrs Geary, having given up her job and thrown herself into running the guesthouse, would be happy with no security for herself in the longer term, particularly after she had a child with him (planned or unplanned). He should have recognised the risk that she would become more and more anxious about her situation and ultimately try to claim that there was some agreement between them in relation to the property and/or the business if he continued to presume that she would do all this for no return. He too could have offered her a business partnership without risking his interest in the guesthouse. As above, he could have offered her the opportunity to acquire an interest in the guest house while preserving his own contribution by Declaration of Trust.

As mentioned earlier, there would in fact have been potential tax benefits for them in being business partners and utilising their combined personal tax allowances or, through incorporation and shareholdings, paying dividends in a tax efficient manner.

If, in the final analysis, Mr Rankine really did not want to offer Mrs Geary anything at all, he should have offered her a contract of employment and a salary to make it crystal clear where they both stood. Had he done that, would Mrs Geary have committed to the relationship in the way she did later? I think it is highly doubtful. Doing something rather than nothing would have saved a lot of trouble for the pair of them.

FORMALISING THE BUSINESS RELATIONSHIP

The business relationship of an unmarried couple running a business together can be formalised by Partnership Deeds, which will set out the rights and responsibilities of the partners towards each other and the business. It can also define the assets that belong or will (on purchase) belong to the partnership. This document would also provide a mechanism for dissolving the partnership in the event of the partners falling out or separating.

Incorporation of a limited liability company to run your business involves registration of the business at Companies House where lists of all companies are recorded. The ownership of the company is determined by the issue of shares. The individuals who run the organisation (The Directors) are also appointed and recorded at Companies House. There are many legal responsibilities involved with being a director and running a limited company[33]. Directors and shareholders can be (and often are) one and the same. The company is responsible in its own right for everything it does and its finances are separate from your personal finances. In law it is like another person and any profit it makes is owned by the company. After it pays Corporation Tax the company can then share its profits through declaring 'dividends' to its shareholders.

Most limited companies are 'limited by shares'. This means that the shareholders' responsibilities for the company's financial liabilities are limited to the value of shares that they own but have not paid for.

Company directors aren't personally responsible for debts the business can't pay if it goes wrong, as long as they have not broken the law (usually this means things like trading while the company is insolvent). Here is an example.

> A limited company issues 100 shares valued at £1 each when it is set up. The two shareholders own 50 shares each and have both paid in full for 25 of these. If the company goes bust, the maximum the shareholders have to pay towards its outstanding bills is £50 - the value of the remaining 25 shares each of them has not yet paid for.

NOTES

[32] [2010] EWCA civ 555.

[33] **https://www.gov.uk/running-a-limited-company**

•11•

Ownership of Chattels/Personal Property

An oft quoted maxim 'possession is nine tenths of the law' has great force in relation to personal belongings as between separating unmarried couples. The simple reason for this is that, almost without exception, the cost of seeking to recover personal possessions from a former partner with whom you are in dispute outweighs the actual value of the item or items concerned. In most cases, it will actually be cheaper to simply replace the item(s) with similar new or second hand items.

With the above in mind, it must be sensible for cohabitees to make some agreement between them about what is to happen to personal possessions in the event of a separation (see 'Cohabitation Agreements' in Chapter 6). That is perhaps wishful thinking in many cases. The blunt fact is that in an acrimonious separation, the party in possession of a particular item often ends up keeping it, unless the other is prepared to agree to pay a price (monetary or otherwise), which is wholly disproportionate to the value of the item, or unless a bargain can be struck to exchange items between the couple.

It is also the case that, sometimes, items of particular value or significance such as heirlooms are in dispute. In these situations, the legal status of these items becomes significant. The following briefly describes the legal principles with regards to original ownership of personal property and the means by which ownership can change between cohabitees.

Personal property (sometimes called 'chattels') actually refers to moveable (as opposed to immoveable) belongings. It therefore includes things such as vehicles and furniture, but excludes houses and land, which are called 'real' or 'immoveable' property. It also excludes things like patents and publications, which are known as 'intellectual' property.

Ownership of personal property rests with the person who originally purchases or creates the item in question. Similarly, where an item is purchased using funds provided by both parties or from a joint account, then the item in question belongs to the contributors to the purchase price. Generally speaking, unless an intention to the contrary can be shown, it will be presumed that a joint purchase is intended to be in equal shares even if the size of the parties' respective contributions differs.

Long term cohabitees can usually divide their personal property into four categories:

1. things I bought;
2. things you bought;
3. things we bought together; and
4. things gifted to me/you/us.

There is usually a degree of co-mingling of property, particularly over a longer relationship. It is also usually the case that each partner will remember pretty accurately which items (or, at least, those which actually matter) they each brought with them to the relationship. In the case of heirlooms and items of personal significance, the position is clear. Legal ownership rests with the person who inherited it, bought it or to whom it was gifted. It is unusual for one partner to agree to part with items of such personal significance to them, although the number of cases of one party withholding items of personal significance to their former partner is depressingly high.

The most frequent cause of dispute between cohabitees about their personal property relates to things they purchased together, things they gifted to each other or things which were gifted to one or both of them by a third party during the relationship. A 'gift' is defined as:

> 'A thing given willingly to someone without payment; a present'[34]

At common law, for a gift to have legal effect, there must be an intention by the giver to give the item, physical delivery of the item to the recipient and acceptance. A promise of a future gift is not enforceable so, for example, it is not possible to say 'you told me last year that you would give the car to me next year, so I am keeping it'. The intention is gratuitous and a matter of choice for the giver, so he or she can always change their mind until the gift has actually been made.

To determine whether a gift has actually been made, there are three basic elements:

1. Delivery - control of the gift must have passed from the giver to the recipient. In almost all cohabitee situations this means the physical handing over of the item.
2. Intention to gift - consideration is given to the words used, the relationship of the parties, the surrounding circumstances and the size of the gift in relation to the giver's resources generally. In other words, the giver must mean it and do it for the right reasons. 'Love' will do just fine as a reason, but the giver must not be under any pressure. There will also be a greater likelihood of the 'gift' being successfully challenged if they are giving away more than they can realistically afford. Therefore, it might be fair to say that the love must be mutual and a partner who is found to be taking advantage may not be permitted to keep the benefits of their partner's misguided generosity.
3. Acceptance - it seems odd to say it, but the recipient must unconditionally accept the gift before it becomes valid.

There is frequently disagreement about gifted items on separation but, if the above principles are rigorously applied, the true situation will emerge.

As to items purchased by the couple jointly, the difficulty usually arises over the 'big ticket' items. There is almost guaranteed to be one item you both want or which is worth more than all or most of the others put together. How best to deal with it? Well, putting aside the maxim with which this chapter commenced, which is almost certain to lead to recriminations and dispute, here are the usual solutions.

- Item plus cash - one partner keeps the item and compensates the other for its fair open market value. How to arrive at fair open market value depends on the item concerned. It is rarely appropriate to use 'new' value for comparison because all personal belongings, with the exception of collectables and antiques, depreciate in value, sometimes quite alarmingly. Second-hand value is usually the best measure. This can be arrived at by comparisons with other similar items advertised for sale or by obtaining a valuation from a buyer's guide or someone in the trade (for example, a car dealership).

- Sell it and divide the proceeds - the 'Wisdom of Solomon' solution may be the only way if you accept it belongs to you both, you both want it and can't agree who will keep it.
- Flip a coin - not fair if there is a single 'big ticket' item, but surprisingly effective where there is more than one valuable item. The coin toss determines who goes first and the process then alternates moving from room to room. A sad but swift process. A trusted and sensible mutual friend is always invaluable in such situations. Keep the lawyers out of this process if at all possible.

NOTE

[34] *Oxford English Dictionary* definition.

◆12◆

Pensions

- One in six pensioners live in poverty (1.8m or 16 per cent of pensioners).
- 1.2m live on the edge of poverty.
- Low income is often linked to earlier low pay/time out of employment such as, for example, caring responsibilities.
- Women are in the higher risk group, along with single people living alone.
- Women get 32p in each £1 that their male partners/husbands get.
- The pay gap during working life gets far larger in retirement.
- The State pension system makes it harder for women (Fawcett Society).
- This is a global problem.
- The poverty rate in the EU for women is 37 per cent higher than for men.
- Women live, on average, five years longer than men – increasing the issue.
- Women are often dependent on a partner for retirement income – but death/separation can end this.
- Women generally receive a lower average income from men in occupational pensions and from state pensions.

THE STATE PENSION

Old system

The old system ended on 5 April 2016. If your state pension age is on or before this date, then you are under the old system.

The full state pension is £115.95 per week (2015-2016). To qualify for the full amount, you need at least 30 years-worth of National Insurance contributions or 'credits' (where contributions are paid by the government during periods of unemployment, maternity leave or caring, for example).

If you are married, you are entitled to a widow(er)'s pension on the death of a spouse. Cohabitees are not entitled to anything.

If you divorce, any state pension difference can and may be taken into account by the courts when looking at pension income. It is possible to take a former spouse's national insurance credits and substitute them for your own, if this improves your situation. This option is not open to cohabitees.

Therefore, as a cohabitee, you have to ensure that you achieve your own rights to a state pension by sufficient national insurance contributions (Class 1, Class 2, Class 3) either paid through work or, if you meet certain rules, for the government to pay them on your behalf. With the end of this system due in 3½ months (at the date of publication), there is little time to make a difference.

It is possible to purchase missing years by Class 3 NIC. Contact HMRC for a quotation[35]. You can go back up to six years but, if your gaps are much earlier (for example, when child caring but not meeting the rules for the government to pay your NI on your behalf) you will not be able to cover this time.

There is a small window until 5 April 2017 that provides an opportunity to purchase a state pension top up (Class 3A). This is generally worth looking at, for most people, but don't assume that everyone benefits. Always compare this with what else you can do with the funds instead and/or how it may affect benefits. You can purchase up to an additional £25 a week.

You can defer receiving the state pension if you chose. There are some benefits to this, with the higher return that the money may receive in the bank/building society.

New system

The new State Pension will be a regular payment from the government that you can claim if you reach State Pension age on or after 6 April 2016. The full new State Pension will be £155.65 per week.

Your National Insurance record is used to calculate your new State Pension. You will usually need 10 qualifying years to get any new State Pension. The amount you get can be higher or lower depending on your National Insurance record. It will only be higher if you have over a certain amount of Additional State Pension.

In 2016-2017, 130,000 men will qualify for the full state pension and 20,000 women will qualify[36]. Women outnumber men by nearly 2:1 in retirement.

As with the current pension, you have the option of purchasing missing years under the Class 3 national insurance contributions and paying for these going forward (see above).

You can defer receiving the state pension if you chose. There are some benefits to this, with the higher return that the money may receive in the bank/building society. However, it is a lower return than those receive on the older scheme.

AUTO-ENROLMENT

Also known as workplace pensions, this is a way of saving for your retirement that is arranged by your employer. They can use a number of different structures for this. However, there are certain rules about how much you and how much your employer need to contribute. You can chose to opt out, but this can lead to long-term risk of poverty in old age.

OCCUPATIONAL PENSIONS

There are two main types – salary related (often called final salary, defined benefit, career average pension) or money purchase pensions (defined contribution).

These pension schemes are generally a trust structure, which means they have specific rules that are laid out in a trust document, and they are managed by a number of trustees (this will vary depending on the scheme). However, some older style pensions and some government pensions have a different structure and you should check your own scheme for accuracy.

Each pension trust may have slightly different rules, so just because you have a number of defined benefit pensions does not mean that you have the same pension rules in each case. Areas that commonly differ include:

1. Definition of a 'dependent'. On death this is up to a trustee to decide (at their discretion); cohabitees may or may not be

excluded under some older style pensions. Check the specifics of your scheme – 'read the small print'.

2. Whether children will receive a pension on the death of the member and up to what age (the maximum is generally 23, unless the child is disabled).
3. Definition of a 'child' (for example, if the pensioner father is not on the birth certificate but has always been responsible for the upbringing). Remember, this is generally at the discretion of the trustees. This is applicable on death.

WHAT IS AVAILABLE IF YOU SEPARATE?

A cohabitee may be treated as a dependent for a widow(er)'s pension but is unlikely to be permitted to share any of the pension should the couple split before the death of the pensioner. Pension trusts will treat you as separate individuals. In other words, if you have remained at home, looking after the children/partner, while s/he works and accrues a nice occupational pension, put bluntly, it is tough luck – if you are not married to him/her you have no recourse to their pension. The sole proviso to this is where you have children together and the pension is already in payment. The income can then be taken into account to provide for your children. However, I believe that a deferred pensioner (someone who has not yet started their pension) cannot be forced to draw on it (if they are old enough) to provide for children and an income that is not yet happening cannot be taken into account.

PERSONAL PENSIONS

Like occupational pensions, these are generally trusts. Also like occupational pensions, unless you are married you do not have recourse to your partner's pension when you split up.

Again, like occupational pensions, generally the death benefit is at the discretion of the trustees (even if the pension owner has left an 'expression of wishes' giving guidance on how they want the pension left). However, under the recent changes in pension law, it is far easier to leave your pension to your cohabiting partner on death and therefore giving the trustees this guidance is important if you want your wishes followed. Equally it is important to change your expression of wishes letter should you split up if this is no longer appropriate. After all, you will not be around to tell people what you meant to do. When making these important decisions remember the welfare/needs of any children of your relationship and the potential rights of your former partner themselves to claim against your estate if you have not made adequate provision for them (see above).

EQUALITY BETWEEN COHABITEES

Often in a relationship one party takes responsibility for short-term money (how much is the shopping, paying the day-to-day bills) and the other considers the longer term funds (pensions, investments, repaying the mortgage). Over time, an imbalance arises between the partners in terms of assets. This is particularly pronounced in pensions and retirement planning.

I have yet to see an unmarried couple separating in later life with equal income (and frequently assets). The effect is always more pronounced where one partner has taken time out of work (for caring, children, etc.) or where one party's career has been prioritised over that of the other.

In marriage this is taken into account should a couple get divorced – the courts have powers to address income inequality. However, cohabiting does not allow for this and therefore the risks on the person who is not planning for the long term in their own name are huge. The longer the cohabitation, the closer to retirement that the split takes place, the more pronounced this gap can be.

What can you do to address this?

1. Ensure that your state pension is always maximised. Pay the Class 3 NIC if necessary. Do not opt out of Class 2 even if you have the option. It could be an expensive mistake.
2. Save for your own pension. Even if you do not work, you can pay up to £2,880 net a year into a pension, with the taxman adding a further £720 into the pension – even if you do not pay tax in the first place. This is (almost) free money.
3. Read the small print of all your pensions – know and understand what you have, as a couple and individually.
4. Don't put all your eggs in one basket – especially if that basket is in another person's name. It is dangerous. At some point one of you leaves, either through choice or through death. Either one could leave you as one of the pensioners on the poverty line.
5. Do not underestimate the value of a state pension. Purchasing this amount of guaranteed income for life is expensive – in many cases it will be worth as much as your half of the house (or more).

6. Pensions are not the only options to save for retirement.
7. Get married – this may not be what a cohabiting person wants to hear, but it is tax efficient and protects the lower earner/ pensioner on death or divorce.

Finally, some of the ideas above are good even if you are not splitting up. After all, a couple has two personal allowances (the amount you can earn without paying tax). Why have all the income in one person's name, and pay more tax?

NOTES

[35] You can ask HM Revenue and Customs (HMRC) to check your National Insurance record. HMRC will then write to let you know if you can make voluntary contributions and how much to pay.

[36] *Neoliberalising Old Age* by John Macnicol (Cambridge University Press, 2015)

◆13◆

We'll Never Agree About Money - What if I Choose to do Nothing?

This is not to be discounted as an option in the right case but, if you decide to carry on as you are with no written agreement between you, there are certain essential safeguards that you overlook at your peril.

ESSENTIAL SAFEGUARDS

Start by reviewing past events and where you are now in the relationship in terms of emotional and practical commitment and financial contributions. Ask yourself the following questions, looking at the situation not just from your own perspective but also (with total honesty) from your partner's perspective.

1. For joint ownership cases, do you or your partner (if you were to ask them) believe that your shares in jointly owned property are already defined? You can check this relatively easily by asking the solicitor who dealt with the purchase or by obtaining a copy of the form TR1, form JO or any bespoke Declaration of Trust from HM Land Registry. For post 1998 purchases, check the 'Declaration of Trust' section at box 11 of the form TR1 (but check whether it is signed and note

the points in Chapter 7 concerning evidence of actual instructions and advice at the time of purchase). If there is no agreement, think about whether it is right to leave matters unresolved or invite your partner to enter into a Declaration of Trust defining your shares.

2. If asked would you both agree that any property held in the sole name of one of you belongs absolutely to that person (i.e. the other would not have any claim to it in the event of a separation)?
3. Have contributions to date in terms of purchasing or improving jointly owned property or paying the mortgage been provided predominantly by one of you?
4. If one of you legally owns property, has the other already contributed to its purchase or improvement so that they may feel (rightly or wrongly in your view) a sense of ownership or entitlement?
5. Is one of you is the 'handyman' type who has carried out work that has improved the value of the property in addition to any financial contribution they may have already made? Is that person likely to feel an entitlement as a result of that?
6. In the case of a business, are you heading for dispute by leaving matters as they are (whether as the present business owner or as the non-owner helping to run it)? Weigh that against the benefits of a partnership or limited liability status defining the extent and ownership of the business assets and maximising your respective tax exemptions.
7. If you are the property owner have you, at any time, acted in a way that may have led your partner to believe they have a financial interest in your property? If you are the one who would benefit most from the legal position staying as it is remember that intentions change, hence the words 'at any time'. Your intentions may have changed since the enthusiastic discussions about shared plans before you started to have doubts. It doesn't necessarily follow that your partner's intentions have changed or that they have stopped relying on the promises and agreements you made back then. In fact, if they are feeling vulnerable, they may cling ever more tightly to the 'promise' they believe they were made. Once the 'deal has been done' and the terms relied on, it is too late to turn back the clock, a fact which many parties to these kinds of dispute find it hard to understand from the perspective of a recent separation.

8. The same principles apply to the non-owning (and consequently weaker) partner. You may think you have been given assurances, which persuaded you to invest time or money, but what would your partner who owns the asset say if asked now?
9. Have you been or are you currently engaged to be married? If not, did the engagement end within the last three years? This is a key indication of commitment in legal terms and, if coupled with 'a significant contribution in money or money's worth to the purchase or improvement of property' by one person (to quote the statute), it can lead to that person acquiring a financial interest or enhanced interest in the property. Do not delay in addressing this if your legal position as a non-owner is weaker than that of your partner.

The answers to the above questions may indicate that the potential for future dispute already exists. Weigh up the risks of leaving things as they are against the benefits of having a 'where do we stand?' conversation with your partner. Consider the points at the start of Chapter 4. You may find that an open discussion about these issues will reveal that you are heading in the same direction or at least able to reset the clock in financial terms and alleviate any lingering concerns. It may also enable you to consider the potential benefits of sharing at least some things.

On the other hand, it may reveal simmering tensions. It is a personal decision for the individual. If you are able to reach some kind of agreement, consider whether a Declaration of Trust, Business Partnership Agreement or Cohabitation Agreement is appropriate. Which of these fairly reflects the situation and will alleviate any anxiety or sense of grievance by either of you? If you conclude that this is not right for you, think about how you are going to record or preserve the understanding you have reached for future reference.

If, on reflection, you decide that things are best left as they are with no attempt at discussion or to enter into a written agreement of any kind, the following are important steps to prevent future dispute and limit the scope for claims based on past conduct.

PREVENTING FUTURE DISPUTES

In the case of the sole owner, the party owning the home, where it is agreed or intended that the other will not acquire an interest, should not permit the non-owner to form the impression that the property is, or might be, or will, become jointly owned by your words or deeds. You should not permit your partner to:

1. Contribute to the mortgage or to the bank account from which it is paid.
2. Pay a lump sum or sums towards reducing the mortgage or the cost of improving the property.
3. Provide physical labour or purchase materials to extend or improve the property. Paying for or working on extensions, loft conversions, bathrooms and kitchen refits are the most common elements of claims to an interest in property.

I frequently give this advice. I have no qualms about doing so for someone emerging from divorce or a previous relationship who wants to protect assets for their children by that relationship. I also see many unmarried people following separation whose former partners have followed similar advice. Often these are long relationships with all the features of marriage including children. The 'non-owning' party has contributed in diverse ways to the relationship and enabled their partner to accumulate wealth and property by their efforts, either through looking after their children, providing emotional and practical support, or helping with the non-property related bills that free up their partner's income to pay for the property itself. I have to advise them that they have no real claim for themselves because their partner has not permitted them to do any of the things that might give rise to a claim.

Obviously it is a matter of personal choice whether to commit to such a relationship, but the worrying aspect is that frequently the disadvantaged partner is unaware of just how few rights they have and they only discover the truth at the end of a relationship to which they have committed everything.

For the non-owning party who is or has been paying towards the mortgage or who has contributed to the deposit or to improve the property (financially or by physical effort), it is recommended that you do not rely on assurances, but rather you should seek some agreement with your partner. Your legal position in the event of a separation is weaker if you do not have a clear written agreement or strong evidence to support any claim. In my view, therefore, 'leaving matters are they are' or 'doing nothing' is inadvisable for you. At the very least you should take stock of where you are now and ask yourself the following questions:

1. What was it about your partner's words or deeds that made you think that there was some agreement or understanding between you about you having a share in the home? It may

have been a discussion about your future plans that made you think you both owned or would, in due course, both own the home although the legal title at that time belonged to him/her. Write it down for future reference. Judges look for evidence of these conversations or actions that might explain why you acted to your disadvantage even though (on the face of it) you didn't own anything. You will be expected to recount the details as accurately as possible if there is a dispute.

2. Are there any witnesses who can confirm this? What would they say if asked? Could you tactfully remind them just in case their evidence might be required later?
3. What documentary evidence is there of what you have spent? Remember the legal obligation for the banks is to retain statements for seven years. Many banks hold records for much longer, but you shouldn't take any chances. Order copies and annotate the relevant transactions for future reference.
4. Are there any receipts/invoices for work and materials? If so keep them together.
5. Do you have photographs of any improvements that have been carried out (especially if they depict you doing the work)? Many people keep 'before' and 'after' photographs. These can, if required, be used to evaluate the uplift in value you have created by your contributions.
6. Is there or was there an engagement between you? If so, has it been broken off within the last three years? This date is significant because three years is the time limit for bringing proceedings under section 37 of the Matrimonial Property and Proceedings Act 1970[37] (see Chapter 16). Don't be fooled by the reference to 'husband' and 'wife' in the statute. It relates also to the formerly engaged.

NOTE

[37] Contributions by spouse in money or money's worth to the improvement of property. 'It is hereby declared that where a husband or wife contributes in money or money's worth to the improvement of real or personal property in which or in the proceeds of sale of which either or both of them has or have a beneficial interest, the husband or wife so contributing shall, if the contribution is of a substantial nature and subject to any agreement between them to the contrary express or implied, be treated as having then acquired by virtue of his or her contribution a share or an enlarged share, as the case may be, in that beneficial interest of such an extent as may have been then agreed or, in default of such agreement, as may seem in all the circumstances just to any court before which the question of the existence or extent of the beneficial interest of the husband or wife arises (whether in proceedings between them or in any other proceedings).'

◆14◆

What if We Decide to Get Married?

Many people worry about the financial implications of marriage, particularly those who have all or most of the assets, those who have had difficult previous experiences of divorce or who have dependents by previous relationships for whom they wish to provide. It used to be the case that the divorce courts would rarely permit married couples to decide what a financial settlement on divorce would look like. Of course this is in complete contrast to the position of unmarried people who are free to make binding cohabitation agreements and declarations of Trust about property as they see fit. However, things have started to change. Recent court decisions have upheld agreements between married couples (known as 'pre-nuptial agreements'). There is even talk of legislation to permit these agreements by Act of Parliament. The following is a guide to these agreements.

WHAT IS A PRE-NUPTIAL AGREEMENT?

A pre-nuptial agreement is a written formal agreement entered into by a couple before they get married that sets out a game plan for what they have agreed will happen to their assets in the event of a future divorce.

Is it enforceable?

Each case will depend on the particular circumstances of the case and the manner in which the pre-nuptial agreement was entered into.

Pre-nuptial agreements are not binding in the Courts in England and Wales. Until recently they had been given little weight. However, more recently the Courts have been prepared to take couples pre-nuptial agreements into account. In one landmark case known as *Radmacher* v. *Granatino*[38] the Court upheld the pre-nuptial agreement.

In order to ensure a pre-nuptial agreement has the best possible chance of being upheld the following should happen as a matter of course:

- full and frank disclosure by each party to the other of their income, capital and pension provision;
- each party be given and have the opportunity to obtain independent legal advice;
- the pre-nuptial agreement should be signed at least six weeks prior to the marriage;
- there must be no undue pressure or undue influence placed upon either party;
- both parties should be in good health;
- the pre-nuptial agreement should make provision for the wellbeing and maintenance of any children, both now or in the future.

When is a pre-nuptial agreement advisable?

A pre-nuptial agreement is advisable:

- if there is an imbalance of the relative wealth of the parties to the marriage;
- where one or both parties have been married before, and come into the new marriage with assets;
- where either party to the marriage has wealthy parents;
- where there is a family business;
- where there is family money that, if the worst were to happen, the family would prefer remains within the family;
- where there are children from a previous relationship, to ensure they receive their intended inheritance;
- where either party has assets that they have built up prior to the marriage.

Should the parties take legal advice?

You do not need to use a lawyer, but there are many dangers if you draw up a document without legal advice.

The cost is minimal compared with the financial protection and benefits you will get from a properly drawn up pre-nuptial agreement.

The Courts in England and Wales can be arbitrary in divorce settlements and are unlikely to have sympathy for a couple who try to rely on a makeshift agreement and where neither party has had the foresight to obtain proper legal advice.

Each person's situation is different and a pre-nuptial agreement needs to be fully and carefully considered.

The actual agreement should be drawn up properly by a qualified family lawyer and be tailored to your individual requirements.

How to bring up the subject?

It can be extremely difficult to bring up the subject of a pre-nuptial agreement with your intended. Pre-nuptial agreements can be seen to be self-serving and can cast a shadow over what is otherwise a happy occasion. Here is some advice on to how to raise the issue.

- Make it clear that any agreement is to protect you both and not just yourself. Explain that you in no way expect a divorce in the future. This is 'just in case', in the same way you do not expect a house fire or a car accident, but you take out insurance to protect you.
- Bring it up early on, before the engagement if possible.
- Ask what it is that your intended knows about pre-nuptial agreements, and answer any questions they might have. You can also make legal advice available to them.
- Make it clear that both of you should have an input when it comes to drawing up the agreement. Make it clear it is not about your intended ending up with nothing.
- Explain that you in no way expect a divorce, but you just want to be prepared and do the right thing.
- Explain that it helps to avoid potential future complications and thousands of pounds of legal costs.
- Explain that it can be a great way to learn more about each other's expectations, dreams and hopes. In some ways it can heighten communication.
- Pick a calm, neutral spot where you both feel you can be open, at ease and unpressured. Ensure that you are in a place where you both feel physically and mentally comfortable.

- Be open, honest and direct. Present it as an ideal to be built on by you both.

Things to avoid:

- do not spring it on your intended;
- do not present it as a done deal;
- do not present it at the last moment;
- do not be overbearing or threatening.

Some conversation starters

- 'Let's talk about our future and what we want. Let's make sure that all our money issues are resolved and then we won't have this hanging over us in the future.'
- 'One thing I have to consider before we marry is my parents' business/money/inheritance. I need to be confident that the business/money/inheritance will remain in the family if the unthinkable occurs.'

NOTE

[38] *Radmacher* v. *Granatino* [2010] UKSC 42.

PART IV

WHAT HAPPENS ON SEPARATION?

◆15◆

Arrangements for Children

On separation, all parents would ideally like to make living arrangements for their children without outside interference. In most cases that is possible, but not all. For those falling into the latter category, there is a remedy available through the courts.

Because the adversarial court system is generally recognised as not ideally suited to resolving issues of this kind, there have been many changes to the process in recent years, all aimed at encouraging parties to settle arrangements between themselves without the need for a solution to be imposed upon them. There are various remedies available.

REMEDIES

Child Arrangements Order

This is an Order regulating when and with whom a child is to live, spend time, or otherwise have contact. Contact can take several forms including indirect contact (for example, telephone calls, letters, cards and presents) and direct contact (i.e. face-to-face and, potentially, overnight contact). There are two forms of direct contact: supervised and unsupervised. Contact could be supervised by a family member, the Local Authority or at a Contact Centre. This is generally a temporary measure and a stepping stone to unsupervised contact.

Prohibited Steps Order

This is an Order that states that a particular action cannot be taken by a parent or by any person without the consent of the Court. This may mean, for example, an Order preventing a person from removing the child from England and Wales.

Specific Issue Order

This is an Order that asks the Court to consider a specific question. For example, whether a child should attend a state or private school, whether a child should receive religious education or medical treatment, or what a child's surname should be.

The foregoing court Orders are known as Section 8 Orders (as they are found in s.8 Children Act 1989). A s.8 Order will end when the child reaches 16 years old or by further Order of the Court.

THE COURT PROCESS

If you find that you need to apply to the court you will need to follow the required process. Before applying you will first of all be required to investigate mediation as a means of resolving the dispute (see Chapter 21). There are a variety of reasons why mediation might not be suitable to a particular situation (for example, urgency, domestic abuse, distance) and, if this is the case, when applying, the applicant must inform the court of the reason why mediation was not tried.

Having reached the court system, you will find that the process is now tailored to early resolution by agreement or order. This is reflected in the terminology used. As a first step the court fixes a First Hearing Dispute Resolution Appointment (FHDRA) date and serves notice on your former partner. This will also trigger the involvement of CAFCASS (Children and Family Court Advisory and Support Service), an organisation that acts as the 'eyes and ears' of the court. The recommendations of an experienced CAFCASS Officer are given great weight by the court.

On receiving details of the application, CAFCASS will carry out checks of police and Local Authority records to find out whether there has been any prior involvement that might affect the welfare of the children if the court were to make an order about their arrangements at the FHDRA.

A CAFCASS Officer (not necessarily the one who will be assigned to the case) will be present at the FHDRA and will meet with you and your former partner usually (but not always) separately to help resolve the dispute. If you can agree matters at this stage then you will simply go before the Court and explain your agreement. The Court may make an Order, but must bear in mind a direction in legislation that no order should be made unless there is a good reason to do so (the 'No Order Presumption'). In other words, you could leave the court with an agreement but no court order to support it, underlining the encouragement for parents to make arrangements for themselves wherever possible.

If you cannot agree at the FHDRA, the Court will probably fix a Dispute Resolution Appointment (DRA). It may also direct a CAFCASS Officer to prepare a report, a process that takes a minimum of 12 weeks in most areas. As part of this, you will be expected to meet with the CAFCASS Officer. He/she may also speak with your children to ascertain their views (depending on their ages and maturity). At the end of this process the CAFCASS Officer will prepare a report recommending what arrangements he/she believes to be best for the children. The report is very important and will heavily influence the court's decision. It goes without saying that it is vital you do all you can to cooperate with and avoid alienating the CAFCASS Officer and that you respect his/her opinion, even if you do not agree with it.

Having received the report, if you and your former partner can now agree, you can ask the Court to make an Order at the DRA. If the issues cannot be agreed the Court will probably fix a Final Hearing, and may direct you and your former partner to file statements about what you want to happen.

At the Final Hearing, the Court may hear direct evidence from you and your former partner, and will decide what Order should be made and, indeed, whether the 'No Order Presumption' applies. The Court may decide that it should make no Order because it will cause further conflict, or because you and your former partner may be able to reach your own agreement.

Throughout this process, the Court's overriding responsibility and concern in making any order is the welfare of the children. In deciding whether or not to make an Order the Court must consider a list of factors known as the 'welfare checklist'.

The Welfare Checklist

- The wishes and feelings of the children. To what extent the children's views will be taken into account will depend upon their age, understanding and maturity.

- The children's physical, emotional and educational needs. This may include looking at the children's medical conditions, religion or education.
- The likely effect of any change in circumstances upon the children. The Courts are keen to preserve the current situation as it recognises that a change in the children's circumstances usually has an adverse effect upon them, but much will depend upon the individual circumstances.
- The children's age, sex, background and any other characteristics that the Court considers relevant.
- Any harm that the children have suffered or are at risk of suffering. Under this comes the issue of domestic violence and child abuse. If domestic violence is an issue you will need to notify the Court at the earliest opportunity (using a specific form called C1A); this is very important because witnessing and experiencing domestic abuse has been shown to have a long-lasting and damaging effect on children throughout their lives. If there has been proven domestic violence or child abuse or an allegation has been made, the Court may order a separate (Finding of Fact) hearing so that the Judge can decide whether or not violence/abuse has occurred. The case will then proceed as usual, but with those findings being taken into account. Domestic violence is not an absolute bar to contact between an abusive parent and his/her children but may affect the way in which the Court deals with contact and the frequency of it.
- How capable each parent is to meet the children's needs (and any other relevant person who will be spending time with them).
- The range of powers available to the Court.

◆16◆

Financial Disputes between Cohabitees

THE FAMILY HOME

The most frequent area of dispute between former cohabitees concerns the family home, whether it is owned jointly or by one partner. In particular, disputes often arise when considering whether the home should be sold and how much each party should receive.

First steps

A vital first step in any dispute is to check legal ownership of any disputed property. Almost all property is publicly registered today at HM Land Registry, a process that has been ongoing for decades whenever land changes hands or is mortgaged. This means there is an electronic record of almost all property in the United Kingdom, who owns it, to whom it is mortgaged and what other rights the land enjoys or is subject to (for example, rights of way over neighbouring property or third parties claiming an interest over the land).

An online search of the Land Registry records by address[39] will reveal the above information and the Title Number for a small fee. You can also find assistance in interpreting the document you obtain on the Land Registry website.[40] For joint owners, one way of establishing swiftly whether the property is held as tenants in common (i.e. if one owner dies, the survivor does not automatically inherit his or her share) is by checking the section of the title document headed 'Proprietorship Register' for the term 'Form A Restriction' and the words 'No disposition by a sole proprietor of the registered estate (except a trust corporation) under which capital money arises is to be registered unless authorised by an order of the court.' In plain English this means that a survivor cannot deal with his deceased partner's share, because that share passes with the deceased's estate. If there is no Form A Restriction entered in this section of the title document, then very probably the property is held as a joint beneficial tenancy, which means the survivor will automatically inherit the deceased's share. I find that people tend to remember if their property has been registered as a tenancy in common, particularly if the shares in equity are unequal (that is not something you are likely to forget), while they often have no recollection if their home is held on a joint tenancy, although the implication of this is that their partner will inherit the whole property should they die and their shares during their joint lives remain effectively equal.

It is also possible to use the Land Registry service to find out if there is any record of agreements about shares in the equity by obtaining a copy of the form TR1, a form JO (if one has been filed) or any bespoke Declaration of Trust. This can be done using another Land Registry form called form 'OC2', which can also be found online.[41] Once this information is to hand you can then consider your position in more detail.

Cases concerning property tend to fall into two broad categories: joint ownership cases and sole ownership cases.

Joint ownership cases

Where both parties are the legal owners of the disputed property, the legal position is generally simpler. If there is a written agreement about their shares in it then that will determine the issue except in very limited circumstances (see Chapter 6). If there is no evidence of any agreement about shares, we have the helpful legal principle that 'equity follows the law' to guide us. This maxim means that while legal fairness does not replace the written law, it backs it up and supplements it. In cases involving cohabitees' rights, it is legally presumed to apply in joint ownership cases so that, where a property is owned by two people, 'fairness' requires a presumption that their shares in the value are also equal unless there is some written agreement between them saying otherwise (i.e. a 'Declaration of Trust'). There is strong legal authority for this.[42]

The exception to the above rule is property that is jointly owned for business purposes rather than as a domestic home and there is no written agreement about shares in the equity. In these cases, shares will usually be determined according to actual financial contribution to the purchase price.[43]

So, we have established that if you are the joint owner of the home who can produce no evidence of an agreement to share unequally you will find it difficult to convince a court that you should be entitled to more of the equity than your co-owner. The notoriously difficult to prove exception to this rule is in the case of fraud or undue influence (see Chapter 7).

In joint ownership cases, following the above guidance will enable you to establish the basic facts relating to the property in terms of ownership and shares in the equity and whether any third party (such as a mortgage company or creditor) has a charge over it.

In cases where it is agreed that one party is going to buy the other out the next step is to establish the value of the equity to be shared. For this you will need to obtain a valuation.

The valuation exercise

The valuation could be in the form of a written marketing appraisal from a local estate agent, or indeed from more than one. This should not cost anything as the agent is hoping for an instruction to sell the property although, of course, if one party is going to buy out the other, there will be no sale. The agent doesn't have to be told this and indeed agents are quite used to being asked to provide valuations in these circumstances and know from experience that if the negotiations fail, they may still end up conducting the sale. Remember to ask for the recommended 'selling' price as well as the 'asking' price. It is the former we are interested in for the purposes of a buyout.

Ideally, to ensure there is trust in the valuation, the exercise ought to be carried out in consultation with your former partner (in terms of choosing the agent) or they ought to be encouraged to obtain their own valuations. Some people choose to obtain two or three and attempt to agree on a figure that represents a fair average.

If a valuation cannot be agreed, then it may have to be attended to (at considerable expense) in later court proceedings, in which case the court will direct the appointment of what is known as a

'Single Joint Expert' (SJE) at shared expense. The rules and guidance relating to appointment of SJEs can be found in the Civil Procedure Rules 1998.[44]

Usually a qualified surveyor is instructed using an agreed letter of instruction. The expert is required by the court rules to acknowledge that his/her duty is to the court rather than to the parties. Nonetheless, it can be difficult at times to agree on the identity of a suitably qualified expert for reasons such as expense, area of expertise and impartiality, in which case the only route to impose an expert on a reluctant party is to seek a direction from the court by applying for a direction to appoint your chosen expert and providing details of (ideally) two or three suitable experts from whom the court is invited to choose one. The Royal Institute of Chartered Surveyors (RICS) maintains a register of suitable valuation experts.[45] It is difficult for a reluctant party to reasonably object to the appointment of an expert from this register.

Single Joint Expert valuations tend to be a little more conservative than marketing appraisals. Estate agents never seem to be able to forget that they want to secure the business of selling the property and a low valuation is unlikely to do that. Experts' fees vary considerably for no apparent reason. As a general rule the larger the property, the higher the fee. For a typical two/three bed residential property, fees should rarely exceed £5-600 plus VAT, shared between the parties.

Once a SJE's valuation is to hand, either party is entitled to ask written questions of the expert about his findings,[46] which the expert is then obliged to answer (often, although not always, for a fee).

Either party is entitled to challenge a SJE's opinion. When court proceedings are up and running, this is done by asking for the expert to attend court to be cross-examined about his findings or, alternatively, by the unhappy party asking the court for permission to instruct his or her own expert. Be aware, however, that involving experts in this way is a costly process, particularly when one considers the expense of their fees for producing or explaining their findings and attending court. It is vital in these circumstances to carry out a careful cost/benefit analysis to establish whether all the money that will be spent on this will be repaid in terms of the additional value that could be created if the exercise is successful, and the risk that it might not be.

Where there are conflicting expert reports, the court will often address this problem by directing that the experts meet and discuss (sometimes referred to as 'hot tubbing') with a view to producing a 'joint statement' of the areas of agreement and disagreement between them.[47]

Once the valuation is agreed or arrived at, the next step is to obtain an up-to-date mortgage statement showing how much you would have to pay your mortgage company if you decided to sell the property. This should include any penalties or early repayment charges. By subtracting the redemption figure from the likely selling price, you will arrive at the 'equity' figure, which represents the true value of the property to the parties.

It is also common for the courts to make an allowance for 'notional' sale costs against the gross value of the property (i.e. ignoring the mortgage), which represents the typical cost of marketing and selling the property. This allowance is often adopted even in cases where one party is buying the other out, for the simple reason that the true value of any property is the sum of money left after deduction of all the usual selling costs and any mortgage. The broadly accepted rate is three per cent although, in an evolving market with online price comparisons and agents offering much reduced commission rates, this figure is likely to come down over time. For a unique property, a local agent is the norm, but for a property with many local comparisons (for example, terraced, semi-detached and flats), a virtual agent (or indeed no agent) is going to be a more frequent choice, so it may be possible to argue against the usual three per cent figure on that basis.

A typical example of the equity calculation for a property with a mortgage of £120,000 is as follows:

Agent/valuer's recommended selling price:	£250,000
Less mortgage redemption figure:	£120,000
Less notional sale costs at 3% of recommended selling price:	£7,500
Equity =	**£122,500** (£61,250 each)

To buy out one party's (equal) share, the other would therefore have to raise £61,250 as a settlement sum (assuming both agree that their shares are equal).

The next (and often most difficult) step in the process is for the party buying out the other to secure a mortgage offer to enable them to take on the mortgage in their sole name and release their partner from liability to the mortgage company. Unless they have access to the funds without recourse to borrowing, they will have to take on a mortgage sufficient to not only continue with the present level of borrowing, but also to pay their former partner their share of the equity. In the example above this would mean a post-buyout mortgage of £181,250 (i.e. the existing mortgage plus the settlement sum). Since the 2008 credit crunch, mortgage lenders have proven decidedly cautious in their approach to lending. The applicant must be able to show a steady income to which the lender's standard multiplier will be applied (rarely more than 4.5 times annual income) and a good credit rating.

Order for sale of (jointly owned) property

Where a property is held in joint names and there is a disagreement about whether to keep it or sell it, either owner can apply to the court for an order for sale pursuant to an Act of Parliament called the Trusts of Land and Appointment of Trustees Act 1996 ('ToLATA').[48] The Act says that the court must take into account several factors.[49] They are:

1. what the owners want to happen;
2. the purpose for which the owners purchased the property (usually as a home for themselves and their dependants);
3. the welfare of any children living there or likely to be living there; and
4. the interests of the mortgage company or any third party with a charge against the property.

For example:

> Bill and Erica own their four-bed home together. They have a mortgage. Their relationship ends and Bill vacates. Erica remains with their three children (two boys aged 6 and 8 and a girl aged 12). Bill wants to sell the home because he has money invested in it and remains liable for the mortgage. Erica objects because she says she can't afford to buy another home for herself and the children with the money she would receive from a sale and would therefore be made homeless or have to rent. Erica says that with the help of State benefits and Bill's maintenance, she can afford to pay the mortgage but can't release Bill from the mortgage account.
> Bill is thinking of applying to the court. He is advised that the court will have to take into account the points 1-4 above. Because they bought the house as a home for themselves and their children Bill is advised that he will struggle to convince the court to order a sale. Erica is advised that it is very likely she can oppose a sale. The house doesn't appear to be larger than she and the children need. She can afford to stay there without the risk of repossession by the mortgage company. It is unfortunate that Bill cannot be released from the mortgage, but he still has his investment in the property that he will receive on eventual sale. Erica is also advised that she has an additional option to oppose Bill's claim. She can apply for transfer of the property for the benefit of their children (see Chapter 17).

Factors that might have made a difference include the size of the property, affordability of the mortgage and cohabitation with a new partner by Erica. If Erica could sell the property and release sufficient equity to satisfactorily re-house the children (and her) as well as releasing some equity to Bill to help re-house him, it might be considered that Bill has a reasonable prospect of achieving a sale. If the mortgage is unaffordable with the income Erica is able to generate (including any child maintenance Bill pays) then Bill might also realistically expect to be granted an order for sale, because otherwise there is a risk of repossession by the lender. It would not be appropriate for Bill's share to remain postponed and for him to remain a party to the mortgage if Erica is living with a new partner at the property.

The effect of delay

When one partner vacates a jointly owned home, leaving the other in occupation, a number of things need to be considered.

1. For how long will the sale be postponed? This ought to be agreed in principle and recorded if possible (for example, the youngest child reaching majority or ceasing full time secondary education).
2. Who will be responsible for the mortgage and insuring the property during the period of postponement of the sale?
3. Should the party paying the mortgage be given credit for their payments and, if so, should this credit be for all payments (including interest and capital) or just reduction in the capital balance? Note, in this regard, the interest represents just the cost of borrowing, so it may be regarded as unfair for this to be set against the non-paying owner's share in the property where the payments are not creating any extra equity. In contrast to this, payments that reduce the capital borrowing are increasing the equity and would be more fairly allocated to the paying party. However, see point 4.
4. Should the owner who has left be entitled to a rent from the other owner? This is sometimes called 'occupation rent' or 'compensation for exclusion'. The non-occupying owner has the right to ask the court to award this rent/compensation under ToLATA.[50] This is at the discretion of the court and the courts are reluctant to award it in most situations, except to the extent that the court will regard the mortgage capital and interest paid by the occupying owner during the period since separation as the equivalent to the other owner's claim for

rent/compensation (i.e. no adjustment either way). There are two possible measures of rent/compensation:

i. one half of the market rental value of the property; or
ii. the difference between the mortgage cost (if any) and the housing costs of the owner who is out of occupation of the property.

The indicators for situations in which the court may be prepared to award rent/compensation are as follows.

1. Where the actual mortgage outgoing is a lot less than the market rental value of the property or the housing costs incurred by the non-occupying owner;
2. Where the occupying owner has excluded the other owner (particularly where the excluded party is looking after the children). Note this requirement arises from s13 (2) of ToLATA which states that:

   (2) Trustees may not;

   a. Unreasonably exclude any beneficiary's entitlement to occupy land, or
   b. Restrict any such entitlement to an unreasonable extent.
3. Where the exclusion has been going on for some time; the court is unlikely to make an award covering a short period where the sum involved is trifling.
4. Has it been made clear by written notice to the occupying party that the other owner considers themselves to have been excluded and that they will seek compensation for that exclusion? In my experience if a judge is conflicted as to whether to award rent/compensation in a particular case, being able to show that notice of the claim has been given can sway that decision in favour of awarding it.

From a tactical perspective, consider the impact on the occupying owner of being told that the other owner wants to charge them a rent. Over time the claim mounts up. It keeps the issue of sale or buyout at the forefront of the occupier's mind because they will know that unreasonable failure to address the issue over the long term can have major financial implications for them.

You may think that it doesn't matter if you do nothing after vacating the property – after all it's still legally yours, isn't it? Well that was what Mr Kernott thought in the landmark case of *Kernott v. Jones*. Mr Kernott moved out of their jointly owned home in 1996, returning 13 years later seeking his share of the value. The following facts were unfavourable to him:

1. He and Ms Jones surrendered their joint endowment policy on separation and he kept the money which he used to buy his own house;
2. He did not show any interest in the property he still owned jointly with Ms Jones over the next 13 years;
3. He stopped paying the mortgage and did not contribute to maintaining the property; and
4. He paid little maintenance for his children who lived with Ms Jones.

Crucially, this was a case where there was no Declaration of Trust establishing the couple's respective shares in the property (see Chapter 6 above). The transfer document pre-dated the TR1 introduced in 1998 in which a Declaration of Trust is included. There was, of course, the legal presumption that 'equity follows the law' (i.e. the house was jointly owned, therefore the shares should also be equal), but the court found (based on points 1-4 above) that since separation the parties shared intentions had changed. It decided that Mr Kernott's share had reduced to 10 per cent of the equity. Had there been a valid Declaration of Trust, the situation would very likely have been different. It is, however, an object lesson for those who think it advisable to simply abandon their property and come back later. Formalities ought to be attended to in case anyone is left in any doubt.

Sole ownership cases (one party owns the home and the other claims a share)

In cases where one party alone owns the property, claims usually arise where the non-owning partner makes some significant contribution either by improving the home or helping to pay for it. These cases are more problematic, legally and evidentially, and consequently more costly to resolve.

Legal ownership of the property by one of you is conclusive unless the other can prove an interest by pursuing a claim through the courts. What the courts are looking for when dealing with these claims is evidence of an agreement between you to show that even though the legal title belonged to one of you, that person agreed that the other would be entitled to a share. It is important to remember that the search for evidence of an agreement is not the same as the search for 'fairness'. Whether the agreement was fair to you both is irrelevant. For this purpose it is enough to show an express agreement (i.e. a written or verbal agreement) or to convince the court that an agreement can be inferred from conduct (i.e. you acted in this way, so there **must** have been some agreement between you even though we can't pinpoint the exact terms or date of it and there is nothing in writing).

Once an agreement is shown, the next element of proving a share is to show that the non-owner relied on the promise to their personal detriment. The legal responsibility for proving these things to a judge rests with the non-owner who wants to be awarded a share. The following quote is from the judge in what remains the leading sole name case (my emphasis):

> The **first and fundamental question which must always be resolved is whether**, independently of any inference to be drawn from the conduct of the parties in the course of sharing the house as their home and managing their joint affairs, **there has at any time** prior to acquisition, or exceptionally at some later date, **been any agreement**, arrangement or understanding reached between them **that the property is to be shared** beneficially. The finding of an agreement or arrangement to share in this sense can only, I think, be based on evidence of express discussions between the partners, however imperfectly remembered and however imprecise their terms may have been. **Once a finding to this effect is made it will only be necessary for the partner asserting a claim** to a beneficial interest against the partner entitled to the legal estate **to show that he or she has acted to his or her detriment** or significantly altered his or her position **in reliance on the agreement** in order to give rise to a **constructive trust** or a **proprietary estoppel**.
>
> **In sharp contrast with this situation is** the very different one **where there is no evidence** to support a finding **of an agreement** or arrangement **to share, however reasonable it might have been** for the parties to reach such an arrangement if they had applied their minds to the question, **and where the court must rely entirely on the conduct of the parties** both as the basis from which **to infer a common intention to share the property** beneficially and as the conduct relied on to give rise to a constructive trust.[51]

This case has come in for some criticism since, in terms of whether the test is too restrictive for the non-owner, but it remains good law.

REMEDIES

The remedies are varied. The most commonly encountered are as follows.

A Resulting or Constructive Trust

If the non-owner is successful, the court will grant him or her an interest in the property. At one time, the courts were in the habit of awarding a share that was based solely on the respective financial contributions of the parties as a proportion of the overall value (for example, 60/40). This rather simplistic approach is known as a 'resulting trust'. No doubt half of unmarried partners in dispute with their former partner would be quite happy with this interpretation of the facts. Very often one party has made a contribution that is non-monetary or is difficult to express in purely financial terms, but is that contribution any less valuable to the couple as a whole? The resulting trust approach has lost ground in decided court cases because it is considered too inflexible to cope with the range of situations encountered in unmarried relationships. As an indication of the extent to which the resulting trust has fallen out of favour we have the recent comments of Lord Justice Etherton:[52]

> Special facts... apply to those living in intimate relationships... they do not normally take legal advice or expect their rights to be reduced to a formal or any written agreement [about] their interests in the family home... those rights and interests must be seen in the context of an enduring, but often changing relationship of interdependency, mutual co-operation, compromise and joint contributions. Those special features are why [it is now] clearly established that the usual concept of a resulting trust does not apply in such a situation... [instead] property rights are to be established by having regard to... what they have said and done over the entire course of their ownership, or where it is clear that the beneficial interests are to be shared but it is impossible to [establish the shares they intended], by imputing the intentions which they would have had as reasonable and just people (i.e. the court makes up an intention about shares for you).

What the judge is describing is a 'constructive trust'. By comparison with its ill-favoured cousin, the constructive trust is alive and well. It permits the court to interpret or infer agreements between the parties about their shares and, in certain circumstances, to simply make them up. The concept is based on either:

1. what the owner and non-owner agreed were their shares; or
2. if there is no agreement about their shares or none can be identified, the court will award an interest which is based on 'a broad survey of the whole course of dealings between them.'[53]

Two things can be divined from this. Firstly there is a great deal of uncertainty about the outcome; it can vary from day to day and judge to judge. Secondly, it is hugely expensive. The quotation 'what they have said and done over the entire course of their ownership' is music to the ears of the lawyer and represents a potentially mammoth evidential task.

For example:

Ben and Lily are buying a home together. Ben has been made redundant and they agreed this presents the ideal opportunity for him to move from his home town to Lily's where they plan to buy together; a fresh start for Ben. He will soon find work there, they think. Lily has £40,000 to put down on their intended house purchase. Ben is able to match this from his redundancy package, but when they visit a mortgage broker they find that Ben can't raise a mortgage because he has no income and a poor credit rating. They discuss and agree to proceed in Lily's sole name. Ben recalls that Lily used the following words: 'It'll still belong to us both equally, it'll just have to be in my name'. Ben remembers feeling reassured by Lily's promise and duly paid his share of £40,000 towards the deposit. On separation, Lily refuses to recognize Ben's interest in the house and claims that it belongs to her outright. She is upset because Ben's contribution to the mortgage turned out to be erratic. In this case, Ben will try to show that there was an express verbal agreement between them and he relied on what Lily said to him - i.e. that he would still have an equal share when he paid the money. He will say that it is a shame he was out of work sometimes, but they both knew he had been made redundant and there was a risk he couldn't pay a full mortgage contribution. He would have done the same had the situation been reversed he says. The crucial elements here are the agreement and the reliance on it by Ben.

Suppose then they made unequal contributions to the purchase and, while they agreed they would each have a share in the property, they didn't agree how much. Point 2. above would then apply. The court would look at all the financial arrangements between them to arrive at a share that represents what it infers they intended.

Proprietary Estoppel

Definition: where the non-owner is given an assurance by the owner of the property about their rights (for example, 'you can live here for as long as you like') on which the non-owner relies to their personal disadvantage (for example, the non-owner gives up their secure accommodation or employent in order to move in with the owner). The person who made the promise then decides to withdraw from it. The court will grant an order if it thinks that it is unfair to permit the person who made the promise to break it. The remedy is the minimum required to compensate the disadvantaged person for the breach of the promise. It is difficult to spot the difference between this remedy and the resulting/constructive trust referred to above (see pages 102-3). The difference is that this claim does not have to relate to a financial interest in the value of the property. It can, for example, relate to a right to live in the property long term. That right has a value, but it is not the same as having a share of the value of the house. This is often used as a 'belt and braces' claim by lawyers where there have been promises or assurances, but they are not necessarily directly referable to the value of the property itself.

For example:

> Carla and Stuart are boyfriend and girlfriend, having met on the internet. They live 200 miles apart and it's getting serious between them. They want to be together. Carla lives in a Housing Association property with a long-term tenancy. She is able to stay there for as long as she wants. She has made it her home with various improvements over the years for which she has paid. She also has a good job in her home town with prospects of promotion. Stuart has his own home.
>
> During a tender moment, Stuart says to Carla: 'Why don't you move in with me? It'll be your home for as long as you want'. Carla duly ends her secure tenancy and moves 200 miles to live with Stuart, leaving her job in the process and taking lower paid work in Stuart's home town.
>
> Two years later, the relationship is over. Stuart hands Carla a notice to quit his property (Carla is not the legal owner and has no tenancy agreement – she has an 'oral license' to occupy which Stuart can revoke at any time).
>
> Note here that Stuart's reference to the property being Carla's 'home for as long as you want' does not, as a matter of law, mean that Stuart intended that Carla would have a share in it. Carla could however claim the right not to be evicted from the home (she is holding Stuart to his promise).
>
> However, it is almost invariably the case in these situations that the claim has to be expressed in money terms as it is no longer possible for the couple to live together. Instead, her claim might be for the money she spent on the home she gave up and the cost of obtaining alternative secure accommodation. She might also seek a sum for her lost earnings due to giving up her secure job for lower paid work to be with Stuart, although it would be assumed that she would be able to adjust in a reasonable period.

It is important to remember that the court also has to balance the benefits a claimant has received from the arrangement against the losses. The role of the court is to do the minimum required to uphold the promise or compensate the injured party for the losses suffered through their reliance on it.

There have been a number of cases involving children of farmers who work long hours for next to nothing on their parents' farms on a promise of inheritance only to be written out of their parents' wills when they fall out. They then ask the court to hold the parents to their promise. These are the classic estoppel cases. The children have not made a direct financial investment in the land itself, but have worked on the land, so a claim in estoppel is the most appropriate remedy.

The principle difference here is that for a claim in estoppel, it is not necessary to rely on a promise or assurance that grants a financial share in the home itself or to show that the claimant has made a financial contribution directly to the other's property.

Section 37 of the Matrimonial Proceedings and Property Act 1973[54]

A formerly engaged partner may claim an interest in their former fiancé's property if they can prove that during the period of the engagement, they made:

> 'A significant contribution in money or money's worth to its purchase or improvement'.[55]

The difference between this claim and the resulting/constructive trust is that it is possible for a formerly engaged person to make a claim even if there was no evidence of express agreement to share property with their former partner. The statute provides that the fact of engagement infers an intention to share. In order to succeed, it must be shown not only that the claimant has made a significant contribution but that the engagement ended within the three-year period before the court action started. It will also be necessary to prove the engagement (see Chapter 18 – Preparation for Making a Claim).

For example:

> William and Kate are very much in love. William proposes to Kate who accepts and they begin discussing the wedding plans. William buys a ring. They have an engagement party to which their friends and family are invited. They live together in Kate's house and agree a date for the wedding. William is a builder by trade and by agreement between them he starts work on a large extension to the house to accommodate the family they plan to have. He does hard manual labour and also spends his money to pay for materials. The extension creates a significant uplift in value of the home. On separation two years later, the engagement ends and William asks for a sum of money in recognition of the work he did. Kate claims that he did it voluntarily and didn't expect anything in return.

The key difference here is that William does not have to prove any agreement between him and Kate that he would receive an interest in the home; that will be inferred from the engagement (a clear intention to share). William will still be required to prove the engagement (relatively simple in the circumstances) and show that he made a 'significant contribution in money or money's worth' to buy or improve the home. He has three years from the end of the engagement to make his claim, failing which he will still be entitled to proceed but has the additional burden of showing that there was an agreement between them. He will be seeking a sum that will probably be assessed as the difference between the value of Kate's house without and with the extension he built and paid for.

NOTES

[39] **https://www.gov.uk/get-information-about-property-and-land/search-the-register**

[40] **https://eservices.landregistry.gov.uk/www/wps/QDMPS-Portlet/resources/example_register.pdf**

[41] **https://www.gov.uk/government/uploads/system/uploads/attachment_data/file/449554/OC2.pdf**

[42] Lady Hale in the case of *Stack* v. *Dowden* at paragraph 69 'At the end of the day… cases in which the joint legal owners are to be taken to have intended that their beneficial interests should be different from their legal interests will be very unusual'.

[43] Lord Neuberger in *Laskar* v. *Laskar* [2008] EWCA Civ 347.

[44] **https://www.justice.gov.uk/courts/procedure-rules/civil/rules/part35/pd_part35#1.1**

[45] RICS Dispute Resolution Service can appoint an independent expert witness in the specialist area required ensuring the expert witness is suitably experienced, impartial, free from conflict of interest and available. For parties that require the President of RICS to make an appointment please contact DRS on 020 7334 3806 or **drs@rics.org**. An application form can be downloaded from **www.rics.org/drs**

[46] Civil Procedure Rules CPR Part 35.6 refers.

[47] CPR Part 35.12 refers.

[48] **http://www.legislation.gov.uk/ukpga/1996/47/contents**

[49] **http://www.legislation.gov.uk/ukpga/1996/47/section/15**

[50] ToLATA s.13 (6) (a) refers.

[51] Lord Bridge in the 1990 House of Lords case of *Lloyds Bank* v. *Rosset*.

[52] *Crossco No 4 Unltd & Ors* v. *Jolan Ltd & Ors* [2011] EWHC 803 (Ch).

[53] *Oxley* v. *Hiscock* [2004] EWCA Civ 546

[54] **http://www.legislation.gov.uk/ukpga/1970/45**

[55] s.37 Matrimonial Proceedings and Property Act 1970.

◆17◆

Financial Provision for Children

It is important to remember that while unmarried couples have absolute freedom to enter into financial agreements that bind them in the event of a separation, this does not extend to dismissal of or limitation on claims for financial provision for their children, be that in the form of day-to-day maintenance or the provision of capital/ property. Claims by or on behalf of children will continue throughout a child's minority and continuing education (including university).

CHILD SUPPORT

If you apply to the Child Maintenance Service (CMS) for payments to be made by your former partner, or your former partner applies for a payment to be made by you (depending on where the children live), the CMS will calculate the amount of maintenance payable, which is then reviewed annually. There are six steps.

Step one: income

The CMS will find out the paying parent's yearly gross (pre-tax) income. The highest amount of a paying parent's gross weekly income that can be taken into account is £3,000.00. If the paying parent's income is more than this, the receiving parent can apply to the Court for extra child maintenance.

If the paying parent refuses to provide information, the CMS may make a 'best evidence assessment' using previous information provided or the Annual Survey of Hours and Earnings,[56] to estimate income for a particular profession. Alternatively, the CMS can make a 'default maintenance decision' of maintenance of £39.00 per week for one child, £51.00 per week for two children, and £64.00 per week for three or more children. The paying parent may therefore have to pay more than they need to until they provide the correct information, or alternatively have to pay extra child maintenance to make up for the amounts that should have been paid before the correct information was provided.

Step two: things that affect income

The CMS will check for things that could change the gross income figure, such as pension payments that are deducted.

Either party can apply for a 'variation'. The paying parent can apply for the CMS to take special expenses (for example, child contact costs, school fees, children with additional needs or the mortgage on the former family home) into account to reduce their gross income. The receiving parent can ask the CMS to look at additional income that the paying parent may be receiving (such as unearned income and income diverted to another person or purpose), which would increase their gross income.

The CMS will then convert the yearly gross income amount to a weekly figure.

The final thing that might affect income would be other children the paying parent supports. These are children for whom the paying parent or their partner gets Child Benefit, whether they live with them or not. This affects the child maintenance calculation if the paying parent has a gross weekly income of between £200.00 and £3,000.00, and is applied as a percentage. There is a reduction of 11 per cent to the gross weekly income if the paying parent supports one other child, 14 per cent for two other children, and 16 per cent for three or more other children.

Step three: Child Maintenance rates

The CMS will then apply one of five rates, based on the amount of gross weekly income. These are as follows:

Rate	**Gross weekly income**
Nil	Less than £7.00
Flat	£7.00 to £100.00 (or receives benefits)

Reduced £100.01 to £199.99
Basic £200.00 to £800.00
Basic Plus £800.01 to £3,000.00 (the first £800.00 of income is taken into account using the Basic rate).

Step four: children taken into account

The CMS take into account the number of children for whom the paying parent must pay child maintenance and any family-based (voluntary) arrangements.

Step five: weekly amount of Child Maintenance

Using information from the first four steps, the CMS make a decision about a weekly child maintenance amount.

Nil Rate – no child maintenance is payable.

Flat Rate – £7.00 per week, regardless of the number of children.

Reduced Rate – £7.00 per week for the first £100.00 of income, plus a percentage of the rest of their gross weekly income as per the following table:

Number of children supported and to be taken into account.	Number of children Child Maintenance must be paid for.	Amount of Child Maintenance payable.
0	1	£7.00 plus 17% of income over £100.00.
0	2	£7.00 plus 25% of income over £100.00.
0	3 or more	£7.00 plus 31% of income over £100.00.
1	1	£7.00 plus 14.1% of income over £100.00.
1	2	£7.00 plus 21.2% of income over £100.00.
1	3 or more	£7.00 plus 26.4% of income over £100.00.
2	1	£7.00 plus 13.2% of income over £100.00.
2	2	£7.00 plus 19.9% of income over £100.00.

Number of children supported and to be taken into account.	Number of children Child Maintenance must be paid for.	Amount of Child Maintenance payable.
2	3 or more	£7.00 plus 24.9% of income over £100.00.
3 or more	1	£7.00 plus 12.4% of income over £100.00.
3 or more	2	£7.00 plus 18.9% of income over £100.00.
3 or more	3 or more	£7.00 plus 23.8% of income over £100.00.

Basic Rate – a percentage of gross weekly income as per the following table:

Number of children Child Maintenance must be paid for.	Amount of Child Maintenance payable.
1	12% of gross weekly income.
2	16% of gross weekly income.
3 or more	19% of gross weekly income.

Basic Plus Rate – the full amount of the Basic Rate, plus a further percentage in respect of gross weekly income over £800.00 as per the following table:

Number of children Child Maintenance must be paid for.	Percentage applied to the first £800.00 of gross weekly income.	Percentage applied to gross weekly income over £800.00 (up to £3,000.00).
1	12%	9%
2	16%	12%
3 or more	19%	15%

Step six – shared care

If care is shared, the CMS will deduct a figure from the weekly maintenance to reflect the average number of shared care nights each week as a proportion of child maintenance paid.

If the day-to-day care of a child is equal between a paying parent and a receiving parent then the paying parent would have to pay no child maintenance for that child.

Flat Rate – if maintenance is set at the Flat Rate because the paying parent's income is £100.00 per week or less, then shared care is not taken into account at all. If it is set at the Flat Rate because the paying parent receives benefits, then shared care of at least 52 nights per year reduces the child maintenance to £0.00 for that child and any other child living in that household.

Reduced, Basic and Basic Plus Rates – the amount of maintenance is divided between the number of children, and then the number of nights each child spends with the paying parent is taken into account, as per the following table:

Number of nights of shared care each year.	Percentage reductions to Child Maintenance (for each child).
52 – 103 nights.	1/7th
104 – 155 nights.	2/7th
156 – 174 nights.	3/7th
More than 175 nights.	1/2 (50%) plus an extra £7.00 per week reduction for each child in this band.

The CMS should be informed of a change in shared care only if it results in a change in the shared care band as set out above. After shared care has been taken into account a paying parent will always pay at least £7.00 per week in child maintenance; the weekly payment cannot fall below this amount.

DEALING WITH THE CMS

In cases where the CMS are asked to carry out an assessment both parents will be notified and may be asked to complete means forms (most usually the non-resident parent) or be asked for further information. If the information is not supplied then a debt will start accruing, and the person who fails to provide the information may also be committing a criminal offence. Where a parent is clearly failing to provide information the CMS can issue a default assessment based on what they think the parent is earning, and can approach their employer to deduct the money from source.

Applying for a change in a decision made by the CMS

If you believe a decision by the CMS is wrong, that the application of the guidelines has resulted in an unfair decision, that a mistake has been made, or there is a change in your circumstances, there are various methods open to either parent to ask the CMS to reconsider (a mandatory reconsideration). If you believe the decision is still wrong, then you can appeal to an independent tribunal.

In some cases you should be aware that parents may not be notified and decisions can be reviewed or changed without your knowledge, and can in some cases be backdated for several years.

For more information, you can visit the CMS website.[57]

THE CHILD MAINTENANCE AND ENFORCEMENT COMMISSION (CMEC)

The CMEC was introduced in 2008 as a result of complaints relating to the collection of child maintenance. Among its roles is the responsibility of collection and enforcement of child maintenance.

The CMEC have been given wide-ranging powers to enable the collection of child maintenance, including deduction from a person's earnings and, with the approval of a court, a Liability Order that can impose a range of enforcement actions including committal to prison, freezing bank accounts and charging/selling property.

TRANSFER OR SETTLEMENT OF PROPERTY BELONGING TO ONE PARTY TO THE OTHER FOR THE BENEFIT OF THEIR CHILDREN

Under Schedule 1 to the Children Act 1989[58] sections 2 (d) and (e), a parent may apply to the court for an order that the other transfers property to them to accommodate their children until they grow up.

These orders are almost always made only until the child reaches 18 years of age or leaves secondary education, at which point the property is returned to the original owner (the other parent). The court must take into account all the circumstances of the case including:

1. the income, earning capacity, property and other financial resources which each parent has or is likely to have in the foreseeable future;
2. the financial needs, obligations and responsibilities which each parent has or is likely to have in the foreseeable future;
3. the financial needs of the child;
4. the income, earning capacity (if any), property and other financial resources of the child;
5. any physical or mental disability of the child; and

6. the manner in which the child was being, or was expected to be, educated or trained.

Claims can be made against someone who has voluntarily assumed responsibility for the child, but who isn't the child's parent.

For example:

> Joanne and Michael live together and have a daughter Jade. Joanne also has a son Liam from a previous relationship. Liam's dad pays no maintenance and has little contact with Liam. Michael is a successful businessman with a good income. He has effectively become Liam's father figure and treats Liam as if he were his own son, including providing for him financially. On separation, he agrees to pay maintenance and provide accommodation for Jade, but is reluctant to assist with Liam's needs. Liam's dad has never been involved and in any case receives state benefits and cannot contribute in any meaningful way. If Joanne wants to make a claim against Michael she can also include a claim for financial help in looking after Liam. In this case, the court will have to consider the points at 1 to 6 above and will also have to consider the following points (7-9).

7. whether that person (Michael in this case) had assumed responsibility for the maintenance of the child (Liam) and, if so, the extent to which and basis on which he assumed that responsibility and the length of the period during which he met that responsibility;
8. whether he did so knowing that the child was not his child; and
9. the liability of any other person (Liam's dad) to maintain the child.

The court must also record in the order that the person against whom the order is made is not the child's father.

The first consideration for anyone considering bringing a claim under this Act should always be whether the paying parent actually has the money/property to meet the claim. Usually, this means ownership of property besides the home where they live and/ or substantial capital/savings. It must be affordable for the payer. Many cases are ruled out on this basis.

For example:

> Sean and Katrina have a child Daisy, aged three, who lives with Katrina following the separation. Sean runs a lettings portfolio and has a good income. Katrina and Daisy are living in rented

accommodation on a six-month tenancy. Katrina wants security for Daisy. She asks Sean to help, but he says that the lettings business is his income and he cannot spare capital or a property. Besides, he says, Daisy is fine living in a rented home.

Katrina applies to the court for a housing fund or transfer/settlement of one of the letting properties. The court finds that Sean's letting business is healthy and he can either manage without a property for now or pay a lump sum to fund a suitable house for Daisy. The court orders Sean to pay a lump sum which is to be used to purchase a house for Daisy (and Katrina) until Daisy reaches 18 or leaves full-time secondary education, or until a further order of the court. Sean will then get the property back. In the meantime Daisy has a home and Katrina will not be expected to pay a rent.

The court also decides who is responsible for maintaining the property. Typically, Katrina would be responsible for things like painting the internal walls and woodwork and insuring her contents, while Sean would be responsible for maintaining the structure (roof, load-bearing walls, etc.) and insuring the buildings.

However, Katrina has a new partner. She didn't tell Sean and is worried he won't like her living in the property with someone else. She therefore asks Sean if he will give her a lesser sum of money but outright (i.e. she won't have to repay it later). There are attractions for Katrina because she gets money outright and doesn't have to worry about Sean telling her he wants his money back because she is living in his house with someone else. For Sean it means that he will pay less and can use the savings to invest in his business. In practice this is the kind of compromise that many couples choose in order to avoid continuing ties.

AN ORDER FOR ONE PARTY TO PAY A LUMP SUM TO THE OTHER FOR THE BENEFIT OF THEIR CHILDREN

These claims are available under Schedule 1 section 2 (b) and (c). A parent can ask the court to order that the other parent pays a lump sum for the benefit of their child. Once again, affordability is a key consideration. There must be ready capital. Also, a lump sum cannot be used as a way to capitalise day-to-day child maintenance into a single lump sum. It must be used to provide for a one-off capital need for the child. Typically, this means things like medical treatment that is not available on the NHS or school fees. It can also include things like a reliable car to transport the child.

For example:

Rhianna and Lennie have two children Lauren and Tia. Lauren suffers from cerebral palsy. She requires regular physiotherapy and wears a body suit to help strengthen her limbs. She benefits from various mechanical aids, some of which are available on the NHS but some are not. Rhianna believes that she would benefit from specialist devices.

Tia is a talented musician. Rhianna wants Tia to attend a private school where there is an emphasis on musical talent and where she believes Tia can realise her full potential.

Both parents want the best for their children, but disagree about funding the cost. Lennie says that Tia can manage at state school and that Lauren's needs can be met with aids and devices available through the NHS.

Rhianna finds the stresses of caring for the children with their differing needs very challenging. She could use some financial assistance from Lennie. She says a more spacious and reliable car would enable her to accommodate Lauren's equipment and Tia's musical instruments and allow her to take Lauren to medical appointments and Tia to regular concert performances.

She says he simply doesn't understand how much it all costs and she thinks he has the money to help if he wanted to. She decides to apply to the court for a lump sum. She is advised that the court may make an order requiring Lennie to help. The things she wants to buy are one-off needs and so are available by way of a lump sum order.

A MAINTENANCE ORDER

These orders are only available through the courts in limited circumstances where the Child Support Agency does not have the power to assess maintenance. This happens in the following circumstances.

1. One of the parents and/or the child is resident outside England and Wales. If the receiving parent and child lives abroad, the application can be made to the courts in this jurisdiction for an order against the paying parent in this jurisdiction.[59] The court will be guided (although not bound) by the Child Maintenance formula when deciding the amount payable.
2. When the absent parent lives abroad and the receiving parent and child live here, the receiving parent may apply to their local court for an order and then approach the REMO (Reciprocal Enforcement of Maintenance Orders) Agency,[60] who will arrange for the documents to be registered for enforcement

purposes in the overseas courts local to the paying parent provided the country concerned has a reciprocal agreement with the agency.

3. A 'top-up' order. Such orders are available where a high-earning non-resident parent earns more than (currently) £3,000 per week gross and is already subject to an assessment to pay the maximum child support under the CMS formula. Obviously, such situations are relatively rare, but if your child's parent is a high earner and the maximum CMS assessment would not enable you to maintain a standard of living for your child which is comparable to that which he/she enjoyed when you were living with his/her father or the life he/she enjoys when he/she sees his/her father now, then this is a useful option to remedy the situation.

Note that these potential claims extend also to claims against the estate of a parent in the event of their death under the Inheritance (Provision for Family and Dependents) Act 1975.

NOTES

[56] **http://www.ons.gov.uk/ons/rel/ashe/annual-survey-of-hours-and-earnings/index.html**

[57] **https://childmaintenanceservice.direct.gov.uk/site/public/gb/!ut/p/z1/04_Sj9CPykssy0xPLMnMz0vMAfIjo8ziTTy8HT0MDIy83X3cLA0cAy1MLCy9PI0M_E31w_Wj9KPwKTGBKjDAARwN9AuyswMBHK_6jg!!/dz/d5/L2dBISEvZ0FBIS9nQSEh/**

[58] **http://www.legislation.gov.uk/ukpga/1989/41/schedule/1**

[59] Children Act 1989 Schedule 1 s.14 refers.

[60] **https://www.gov.uk/child-maintenance-if-one-parent-lives-abroad/paying-parent-lives-abroad**

◆18◆

Preparation for Making a Claim Regarding Property

To present your case your solicitor will have to conduct a detailed investigation. You will be asked to provide information about the following matters.

SOLE OWNER CASES

Your solicitor will want a written statement giving a full history of the significant events in the relationship including conversations between you and your partner when you discussed and agreed your future plans. We come back to the quote from Lord Bridge in the Rosset case in Chapter 16. The search is for 'evidence of express discussions between the partners, however imperfectly remembered and however imprecise their terms may have been'. In sole-ownership cases, the exercise is front loaded so that the case should be almost ready for a trial before the issue of proceedings. The solicitor must be cautious and wait until they can consider all the evidence to assess the merits of the claim. Caution is required because the general rule is that, once a claim is issued, the loser pays the winner's costs. It is expensive to start the claim and still more so if you have to pay your opponent's costs. If you want to withdraw, you can only do so with the judge's permission and an agreement or order about who is responsible for the other party's legal costs. It could be your responsibility.

Where there is evidence of an agreement to share or one can reasonably be inferred from your and your partner's conduct, but no evidence of what your respective shares should be, your solicitor will want evidence of the 'whole course of dealing' between you (mortgage/bank statements, responsibility for domestic bills and other outgoings such as repairs and improvements) so as to advise you of the likely share which the court will find you both intended.

JOINT OWNERSHIP CASES

Your solicitor will want to establish if your case is just about whether the house should be sold or if there is also a dispute about your shares in it. This makes a difference to the advice given and the remedy that you will be asking for if you have to apply to the court. It also makes a difference to the procedure used (and likely costs). If the question to be put to the court is only whether the property should be sold or not, there is an accelerated procedure known as Part 8 of the Civil Procedure Rules.

In cases where the issue is only about sale/no sale, your solicitor will ask questions to address the points 1. - 4. under the heading 'Order for sale (of jointly owned property)' in Chapter 16 because those are the factors the court will take into account.

If there is also a dispute about your shares in the value of the property, the solicitor will want to know if there are any agreements about this such as Declarations of Trust. If you are unsure or cannot produce a copy, they will make enquiries at the Land Registry seeking a copy of the form TR1, form JO or any bespoke Declaration of Trust registered with the title (see Chapter 6). They may also make enquiries with the solicitors who acted for you both when you purchased the property, from whom they will want to obtain a copy of the conveyancing file. They will be looking for letters, documents and attendance notes that confirm advice given to you and your former partner about your options to hold the shares in the property and any record of the instructions you gave to the solicitor after you heard their advice. This will help your solicitor to advise you about your share in the property. Remember, it is not about what is fair, but about what was agreed. If, after completing these enquiries, the solicitor can find no evidence of any agreement about shares in the property, they will ask you to provide a written statement covering the points referred to under the heading 'Sole ownership cases' above.

SEVERANCE OF A JOINT TENANCY

If you hold the property as joint beneficial tenants, your solicitor will also want to discuss with you whether you want to sever the joint tenancy. You will recall from Chapter 7 that there are three forms of ownership of real property:

1. joint beneficial tenants;
2. tenants in common in equal shares; and
3. tenants in common in unequal shares.

Very significantly for an unmarried person, the joint tenancy means that if they or their partner die, the deceased's share will pass automatically to the survivor and will not form part of the deceased's estate. After separation you might want to ensure that, if you died, your share would no longer go to your former partner but to your relatives or children. You can do this by serving a simple notice called a Notice of Severance. You will need proof of posting to your former partner to and keep a copy. You should then complete a Land Registry form SEV1[61] and send it to the Land Registry. The effect of this will be to create a Tenancy in Common (divided shares – the survivor keeps his/her share and deceased's share goes to his/her estate).

There are three very important considerations when deciding whether to serve a Notice of Severance. Firstly, what if you and your former partner have young children together? You might prefer that, if one of you were to die, the survivor would have the deceased's share to provide a home for the children and (in due course) to pass on to them through his/her will.

Secondly, what if it is your partner who dies first? Severing the joint tenancy will then deprive you of their share and if you are looking after the children that would be unfortunate. Ages and states of health should be borne in mind.

Finally, when severing a joint tenancy, it is important that you make a will or review your existing will to ensure that your share of the property (which will now pass with your estate) goes to whomever you want to benefit.

When a joint beneficial tenancy is severed the resulting shares in the equity are equal unless and until a court declares otherwise.

STEPS COMMON TO ALL CASES

Your solicitor will seek valuation evidence for any disputed property. In cases where one party alleges work has been carried out and paid for by them, any uplift in market value generated must be valued and evidence obtained of the actual cost involved (for example, receipts and bank statements) and the party who paid (see Chapter 16, section on 'The valuation exercise').

In the interim, your solicitor will consider what steps might be required to protect your position. If your partner owns the property, they could sell it, mortgage it or transfer it without your agreement. Indeed, they might be planning to do so to avoid your claim. Your position can be protected by application to HM Land Registry for what is known as a Restriction against Dealings.[62] If granted, this will place anyone who wants to buy the property (or who is being asked to lend a mortgage against it) on notice that there is a pending claim because the Land Registry will place a notice on the public title register to this effect. In the relatively few cases where the land is unregistered (i.e. there is no electronic record held by the Land Registry), an application will need to be made for a Class 'F' Land Charge using Form K2.[63]

Once the information is gathered the solicitor makes contact with your partner to set out the nature of the claim and invite a response. This process follows what is known as the General Civil Pre-Action Conduct.[64] The process involves a full disclosure being given of the nature of the claim and what remedy the claimant seeks. Disclosure of evidence at this stage is strongly encouraged. The purpose of this is to ensure that each party understands the other's case and that the legal and factual issues can be identified. If either party fails to follow this procedure carefully, they may not recover their legal costs or indeed might have a costs order made against them and in favour of the other party. The reason for this is that the court is specifically required to take into account the extent to which the parties told each other about their case when deciding whether to make orders for costs.[65]

Alternative dispute resolution should be explored before the case is started and considered at intervals throughout (see Chapter 21). This is also important because, should your case go to trial without exploring this option, the court may be asked to take this into account (i.e. the case might have settled if it had been considered, so why should the party who refused/neglected to do so recover their costs?).[66]

PREPARING FOR THE MEETING WITH YOUR SOLICITOR

Proof of evidence

Your lawyer will find it very helpful if you prepare a short written statement setting out facts and figures and the important events in your relationship (a chronology). The following is a (non-exhaustive) list of relevant points to include.

1. Your/your partner's ages.
2. Your children's names and dates of birth (including children by other relationships).
3. Dates of cohabitation/separation.
4. Any health issues affecting any member of the family.
5. Describe briefly any history of domestic abuse in your relationship and whether there has been any involvement by outside agencies such as Children and Young people's Services ('CYPS') or the police.
6. The present and proposed arrangements for the children (for example, the time they will spend with each parent, schooling and any other relevant details.
7. The present financial arrangements between you (occupations, income, property ownership, values, mortgages, other capital and assets, debts).
8. The nature of the dispute between you. If you are a non-owner hoping to claim an interest in a property held by your former partner, you should write down information covering the points referred to in Chapter 13 ('Sole Owner Cases – points 1-8).
9. What do you want your lawyer to help you to achieve?

Documents

Take the following documents to your appointment.

1. Proof of identity. All solicitors will ask you for this. A photographic item such as a driving licence and a domestic bill will usually suffice. You will need to take it to your first meeting.
2. Any legal documents you have received from your former partner or his/her solicitors such as letters, summonses, notices, etc. Check the documents first to see whether there are time limits and make your solicitor aware when setting up the appointment.
3. Any existing court orders such as orders settling the arrangements for your children.
4. Property valuation evidence if you have it (for example, marketing appraisals).

5. An up-to-date mortgage statement showing how much you pay each month and the balance payable on your mortgage account.
6. Evidence of any domestic abuse in your relationship (police logs, referrals to CYPS or Domestic Abuse support organisations), this will be required if you wish to be assessed for legal aid.

NOTES

[61] **https://www.gov.uk/government/publications/form-a-restriction-application-to-enter-sev**

[62] **https://www.gov.uk/government/publications/notices-restrictions-and-the-protection-of-third-party-interests-in-the-register/practice-guide-19-notices-restrictions-and-the-protection-of-third-party-interests-in-the-register**

[63] **https://www.gov.uk/government/uploads/system/uploads/attachment_data/file/396675/K02.pdf**

[64] **https://www.justice.gov.uk/courts/procedure-rules/civil/rules/pd_pre-action_conduct**

[65] Civil Procedure Rules 1998 Rule 44(2)(a)(i) refers.

[66] Civil Procedure Rules 1998 Rule 44(2)(a)(ii) refers.

◆19◆

Funding Options

Whatever funding option you choose, your solicitor is professionally obliged to explore your situation, to provide you with details of the options available to you and their charging rates and terms and conditions of payment. They should also provide you with an estimate of the likely total cost of your case and keep that estimate under regular review. If your case becomes more expensive than at first anticipated your solicitor must inform you of this and the reasons for the increase, and provide a new estimate for the likely overall costs or the next phase of the case.

PRIVATE CLIENT

The private client hourly rate remains the most common method of payment. Most solicitors bill monthly based on the number of hours chargeable time spent on the client's case in the preceding month. Disbursements such as court fees and barrister's fees will need to be paid up front in addition to solicitor's fees. There will be periods when your bills are higher, such as at the start of your case, in the run up to court hearings and prior to a final trial (if required).

LITIGATION LOANS

With the well-publicised decline in the availability of legal aid (see below), commercial lenders are coming to the marketplace. They will fund the case, but for a price. Interest is typically around 18 per cent per annum and is compounded on the sum drawn down by the solicitor over the lifetime of the case. The total plus interest and an 'arrangement fee' is repayable from money recovered in the litigation. The lender will want to take a charge over property (usually the disputed asset) belonging to you if the funds are not paid immediately. They will only advance funds if they can see a clear route to payment and sufficient equity to protect their position.

Even if you do not recover enough to pay your litigation lender (for example, if you lose the case or the asset is not worth as much as expected) you will still remain liable to your litigation lender. Some litigation lenders now offer insurance against non-recovery of costs if, for example, the disputed assets recovered are not sufficient to meet your solicitor's bill, which would ensure that your solicitor is paid, but the insurer will retain the right to pursue you for the insured sum. They will also want to see a reasonable credit score as a precondition for lending you the money to make the claim. It is an expensive way to litigate and should only be considered where there is no other option.

CONDITIONAL FEE AGREEMENTS AND DAMAGES-BASED AGREEMENTS

More commonly encountered in personal injury claims, these agreements are likely to become a feature of cohabitee property and finance litigation. The principle behind these agreements is that the solicitor is paid only in the event of recovery/success and is consequently entitled to charge a 'success' fee or to share with you a proportion of the benefit of the money or property recovered. This uplift recognises the solicitor sharing the risk with you.

Such arrangements are fraught with potential difficulties in cohabitee litigation. Your case will have to be very good indeed if your solicitor is to be prepared to entertain such an arrangement. One issue that will affect that assessment is, bluntly, the possibility of your reconciliation with your partner when the proceedings are well advanced. Your solicitor may have done a great deal of work and wouldn't be paid in those circumstances, unless there is a safeguard in the agreement.

LEGAL AID

It hasn't completely gone away, but the conditions of eligibility have expanded so that fewer people now qualify. You can still get legal aid if:

1. you have a good case; and
2. you qualify financially (find out by visiting the Legal Aid Eligibility Calculator[67]); and
3. you can provide documentary evidence that you or your children are victims of abuse from your former partner. The list of evidence of abuse which will be accepted for legal aid purposes can be found online.[68] Your doctor may have records of treatment you received for domestic abuse. Alternatively, Social Services may have records of assessing you or your children as being at risk of or victims of abuse from your former partner. If so, in Resources 6 and 7 you will find standard letters, which you can adapt to your circumstances, to send to your doctor or Social Services to satisfy the requirement of documentary evidence. You will need to take the letters with you when you go to see your solicitor.

You will also need to take to your solicitor the following documents:

1. Your last three payslips;
2. Your last three months' bank statements for all accounts you hold;
3. Evidence of any savings, investments or valuable items you have; and
4. Letters/notifications from the Benefits Agency confirming how much you receive in State benefits such as Child Benefit, Child and Working Tax Credits and disability benefits.

Your lawyer will help you to apply for legal aid at an early stage if your case has merit and you qualify according to the criteria. Applications for legal aid are now made online. If you want to get the best out of the legal aid system and ensure that your case progresses quickly, you will need to help your solicitor to help you. One of the greatest causes of delay in legally aided cases is in processing the client's legal aid application. It is vital that you get all your documentation together at the first attempt so that your application is not delayed. If information is missing, this often results in the existing information having to be updated and repeated delays in processing your application.

If your case is particularly urgent your solicitor may be able to make a decision to grant you legal aid there and then. This is called 'exercising devolved powers'. To do this the solicitor needs to decide whether your case satisfies certain criteria. You will still be expected to cooperate with the process of assessing your means and satisfying the other requirements and, if you fail to do so, your legal aid funding may be revoked, in which case you may be required to pay the legal costs incurred to the Legal Aid Agency.

If your case is about money or property, you will be expected to repay your legal costs from any money or property you recover or preserve with the benefit of legal aid.

NOTES

[67] http://civil-eligibility-calculator.justice.gov.uk/

[68] https://www.gov.uk/legal-aid/domestic-abuse-or-violence

◆20◆

Domestic Abuse

These issues affect the unmarried every bit as much as those who are married. The impact of domestic abuse on the victim is so overwhelming that it can be very difficult to appreciate what is the right thing to do to protect yourself and your dependents financially at the time of separation unless steps are first of all taken to protect yourself and your dependents physically and emotionally.

The term 'domestic violence' is a misnomer. It encompasses a range of behaviours that may be found in varying degrees in a surprising number of relationships. The cross-government definition of domestic violence and abuse is:

> any incident or pattern of incidents of controlling, coercive, threatening behaviour, violence or abuse between those aged 16 or over who are, or have been, intimate partners or family members regardless of gender or sexuality. The abuse can encompass, but is not limited to:
> Psychological;
> Physical;
> Sexual;
> Financial; and
> Emotional.
>
> **Controlling behaviour**
> Controlling behaviour is a range of acts designed to make a person subordinate and/or dependent by isolating them from sources of

support, exploiting their resources and capacities for personal gain, depriving them of the means needed for independence, resistance and escape and regulating their everyday behaviour.

Coercive behaviour
Coercive behaviour is an act or a pattern of acts of assault, threats, humiliation and intimidation or other abuse that is used to harm, punish, or frighten their victim.

The very many people who experience domestic abuse in their relationships marvel at the ability of a lawyer to speak in such dispassionate terms about their 'remedies' and 'rights'. Long-term domestic abuse, at its most extreme, takes away the ability of the sufferer to even appreciate that they are not at fault for what is happening to them, let alone address the finer points of the separation arrangements. When one considers the conflict between experiencing long-term abuse from the partner you love while trying to make things right and avoiding (24/7) the triggers to abuse, it is hardly surprising that victims find it difficult to end their relationships. The fear of change (when you have been convinced that you couldn't possibly manage if you were on your own) and the thought of your partner's reaction to the defiant act of independence you are considering can cause extreme anxiety.

Research reveals that the number of incidents a victim will suffer before contacting the authorities or support groups is staggeringly high, which is an indication of how conflicted victims feel about their situation. It is also a sad fact that many victims find an unsupportive response so off putting that it can be many years before they finally find the strength to report the abuse again.

I do not pretend that it is easy to summon the courage to address these issues, but once you have made the decision there are a number of things you can do to make the process easier.

Contact a support group. There are groups in your locality. You can find out where they are from the National Domestic Violence Helpline.[69] They can help you with emotional and practical support such as counselling referrals, help with state benefits, housing and accessing competent legal advice. They also offer very insightful courses. In my area a support group offers what is known as a 'Pattern Changing' course, helping long-term victims of domestic abuse identify and understand the pattern of abuse that has become such a familiar and accepted part of their lives. The ultimate goal is to give the victims of domestic abuse the tools and the knowledge to spot the signs and avoid repeating those patterns in subsequent relationships. People I have spoken to who have attended the course describe it as enlightening and empowering.

When you feel ready, there are various legal options available.

NON-MOLESTATION ORDERS

These orders prohibit one partner from molesting the other. 'Molestation' encompasses a range of behaviours including violence, pestering, harassing, mental, physical, sexual, financial, emotional and psychological abuse. Disobeying an order is a criminal offence and the other party may be arrested and brought before the court. If they are found guilty of the breach they may be liable to a term of imprisonment and/or a fine. Either the police can take criminal proceedings or you can take the matter back to the Family Court, depending upon the circumstances of the breach. If the situation is serious enough, the court may be prepared to make an order without notice to your partner to protect you until the case comes back before the court when he/she has been served with the interim order.

THE CRIMINAL OFFENCE OF 'CONTROLLING OR COERCIVE BEHAVIOUR'[70]

The offence, under section 76 of the Serious Crime Act 2015, came into force on 29 December 2015 and carries a maximum sentence of five years and/or a fine. The main elements of the offence include behaviour that:

1. is controlling or coercive;
2. is part of a repeated or continuous pattern;
3. has had a serious effect on the victim or a substantial adverse effect on the victim's day-to-day activities; and
4. was known or ought to have been known by the perpetrator to have a serious effect on the victim.

INJUNCTION AND DAMAGES UNDER THE PROTECTION FROM HARASSMENT ACT 1997

The offence of harassment under the Act is as follows:

> (1) A person must not pursue a course of conduct—
> (a) Which amounts to harassment of another, and
> (b) Which he knows or ought to know amounts to harassment of the other.

This remedy can be used by the police to bring criminal charges and seek a Restraining Order. It can also be used by an individual to take another individual to a civil court for a Restraining Order.

What is often overlooked is the right of the victim to claim damages from their abuser using the same legislation and as part of the same action. One of my colleagues recently acted for a client in such a claim. Our client was awarded damages of £15,000 from her former partner in addition to her legal costs against her abuser in respect of a two and a half year campaign of text and e-mail threats. The total claim accounted for his entire interest in their property.

Damages are awarded in bands according to the seriousness of the abuse. They are as follows:

Less serious cases:	Up to £6,000;
Moderately serious cases:	£6 – £18,000;
Most serious cases:	£18 – £30,000

Only in the most serious cases will compensation exceed £30,000.

If there is a criminal conviction (which there often is in such situations), the abuser will have no defence to the damages claim, which means that the only task for the court will be to summarily assess the level of damages payable.

An injunction order usually expires after a few months, save in the case of very serious long-standing behaviour. An award of damages remains in force until it is paid and the victim (or 'judgement creditor' as they will become) can enforce at any time without notice to the abuser – an important consideration when seeking to deter an abuser. Damages can be enforced by a variety of methods including deduction from earnings, charging/forcing sale of property, bankruptcy and bailiff's warrant.

In addition to risking imprisonment for breach of an injunction, an award of damages will cause even the most determined abuser to take stock in the face of possible loss of assets and income. For those who show contempt towards court orders and/or police action, a hit in the pocket can have the desired effect.

OCCUPATION ORDERS

This is where one party's right to occupy the property is suspended or restricted. These orders can be made in relation to jointly or solely owned or rented property. Generally speaking, orders are made where one party is abusing the other, but this is not always the case. Such behaviour can include abuse of the children living there, whether directly or by being exposed to one parent abusing the other. Even if there is no bad behaviour the court still has discretion to make an order (for example, if repossession by the mortgage lender is imminent and one partner won't sell or leave). A power of arrest can be attached to an order, which means that if the other party disobeys the order they could be arrested. The court must look at other things besides bad behaviour when deciding whether to make an order. Those factors are:

1. both partners' housing needs and alternative housing which might be available to them;
2. the housing needs of their children;
3. both partners' income, savings and other assets; and
4. the judge will ask himself who will suffer the most if he makes an order or doesn't make one. This is called the balance of harm test, and is best explained by an example.

For example:

> Melissa and James live together in a jointly owned property with their two-year-old daughter Ruth. James drinks too much and, when drunk, he is often abusive to Melissa although, to date, he has not used physical violence. James behaves like this in front of Ruth who is frequently upset by her father's shouting. The final straw for Melissa occurs when James pushes her during an argument as she is holding Ruth, causing her to fall with Ruth in her arms. She applies for a non-molestation order and an occupation order. She wants the judge to tell James to leave the home. James is managing to hold down a job and has some spare savings. His parents live nearby and have a spare room. In this case, the judge has no difficulty in making both a non-molestation order and an occupation order because of the way in which James has behaved and because Ruth has been exposed to this conduct. He has alternative housing and some spare cash. He can afford to move out. Clearly, James will suffer no great hardship if he is asked to leave compared with the benefits for Melissa and Ruth of being relieved from experiencing James' behaviour.
>
> Consider now the situation where James is unemployed and has mental health issues that may be made worse if he has to leave. His GP confirms this by letter. He has no relatives or friends living nearby. Add into the mix the fact that Melissa's parents, who regularly look after Ruth, live nearby and would be prepared to help out. The judge's decision about who suffers the most if an order is made compared with no order being made becomes much less clear cut.

When applying for an occupation order there are some 'tactical' points to bear in mind for unmarried partners. Firstly, if the property you want to exclude your partner from belongs to them and not you, then the court can only make an order for six months, which can be extended once for up to a total of 12 months. In addition to the points above, the court has to take some other things into account. They are:

1. the nature of your relationship and the level of commitment involved in it (by both of you);
2. the length of time you have lived with each other;
3. whether you have any children together or living with you;
4. how long is it since you last lived together (if one of you has already vacated); and
5. whether there are any other court cases between you about financial provision[71] for your children or the house itself.[72]

The significance of point 5. above is that if you have started or are about to start a claim for an interest in the property or a claim in estoppel,[73] getting an order from the court that will permit you to live in the property (and possibly exclude your former partner) will hopefully give you the time to conclude your claim. This is important for a number of reasons.

- It concentrates minds. If the non-owner has been given a right to live there along with the owner, it serves as a daily reminder that things won't get back to normal until the claim is sorted out.
- If the owner is excluded, they will incur the cost of living elsewhere in addition to the legal cost of dealing with the claim, and in the knowledge that their former partner is living in the house to which they want to return. This is also a powerful incentive to settle.
- If the non-owner is not able to live in the property, their only leverage to settle is to attempt to negotiate or issue a court claim. They have to find the money for this as well as accommodating themselves (and possibly children) elsewhere. In my experience, if you can stand the short-term discomfort of living in the same property as your former partner or asking the court to exclude them, you are more likely to achieve a favourable financial settlement. Of course you will weigh this against the welfare of your children. If you are advised that, even though your home situation is unpleasant, it isn't so bad that the court will make an order against your partner, then you may think the general wellbeing of the children is more important than having them live in that situation for the sake of achieving a better deal. It is a personal choice depending on your personal situation.

For the sole owner who wants to exclude their non-owning former partner, the above considerations apply in reverse. Your partner, as a non-owner (with no tenancy agreement) has no right to live in your property. Unless and until the court orders otherwise, their occupation depends on an oral licence granted by you when they first moved in. This can be ended at any time by serving a written notice to quit, giving them a reasonable period to vacate the property. If they fail to leave, you are entitled to exclude them.

Of course, taking this step has its hazards because you are forcing your former partner into a corner (for the reasons described above). They may feel they have no choice but to apply for an occupation order or to start a court claim for an interest in the property as a response to this. There could be cost implications if the court is persuaded that you acted improperly. A safer but (at least initially) more expensive alternative is to apply to the court for an order for possession of the property from your partner on the basis that he/she is occupying it 'without your licence or consent'. Your partner will be faced with the choice of leaving or counterclaiming for one of the remedies referred to above or in Chapter 16. Either method will bring matters to a head. You have the advantage that this can be done at a time of your choosing. However, always take advice before serving a notice to quit or enforcing its terms.

NOTES

[69] **http://www.nationaldomesticviolencehelpline.org.uk/** or **http://thisisabuse.direct.gov.uk/**

[70] **https://www.gov.uk/government/uploads/system/uploads/attachment_data/file/482528/Controlling_or_coercive_behaviour_-_statutory_guidance.pdf**

[71] See Chapter 17 - Financial Remedies for Children – Transfer or settlement of property for the benefit of children.

[72] See Chapter 16 – Sole Ownership Cases – Remedies.

[73] Again see Chapter 16 – Sole Ownership cases – Proprietory Estoppel.

◆21◆

Alternative Dispute Resolution (ADR)

In a family relationship context ADR is often referred to as 'mediation'. In unmarried cases, ADR can take different forms depending on the nature of the case. Most frequently used (and cheapest) is 'family mediation' where a family specialist solicitor mediator runs the sessions, which usually take place between the parties face to face. The process is 'steered' by the mediator, but decisions are made entirely by the parties. This method is most often used in trying to agree arrangements for children or financial cases involving jointly owned property which is or was the parties' principle home.

In finance cases that have a more commercial flavour or that are factually complex, a specialist mediator (such as a barrister or retired judge) can be engaged and these sessions are usually attended by the parties and their legal representatives. This form of ADR is more expensive and, generally, the mediator will adopt a more interventionist role, challenging the parties and 'reality testing' their positions in much the same way as the court might do, but in a 'safe' mediation environment where there are no risks of costs, orders or terms being imposed against either party's will.

However strong your case might be, there are risks associated with going to court, particularly if you are an unmarried person with a financial dispute because the court rules (which determine claims between the unmarried) usually require to 'loser' to pay the 'winner's' costs. The cost of going to court can be very high and court fees in particular are increasing year on year. It is essential to stand back and consider the risks, the likely cost to you, and the potential benefits of proceeding. Part of this process of review should involve looking at other options to help you resolve the dispute, such as ADR.

Very importantly, if your financial case does not settle before trial the court must consider the efforts made before and during the case to settle the dispute when deciding how to deal with the question of costs. This includes whether either party was prepared to explore ADR.[74] A successful party who refused to consider this option may be denied some or all of their costs. In almost all financial cases now, the court will routinely order a 'stay' in the court proceedings before trial when it will expect the parties to investigate settlement options including ADR. It pays therefore to look at this option at an early stage. For all the above reasons, you may find that your opponent is actually quite open to the idea of considering ADR. A party who is not may incur the displeasure of the court at a later stage.

Alternative Dispute Resolution is a useful tool in trying to avoid or settle an expensive court process. If a party wishes to make application to the court for a child arrangements order or an order for financial provision for children, mediation must have first been considered. In fact, the court application forms require the applicant to either meet with a mediator before applying (the mediator must then sign the form) or to state one of a number of reasons why they consider themselves to be exempt from the requirement to attend mediation. It is important to remember that mediation is not compulsory for either party, so a party applying to court who does not wish to mediate will only have to show that he/she has seen a mediator and discussed the process. The mediator does not have to declare the process to be unsuitable (although a party who rejects mediation without good reason may come in for criticism).

It is equally important to remember that mediation is not suitable in all cases. Examples of situations that might render the process unsuitable or at least require thought about safeguards include:

1. where there has been actual or threatened domestic abuse or child abuse;
2. where one party remains too emotionally involved to approach mediation in a constructive manner;
3. where one party is simply using the process to delay resolution;

4. where there is a significant inequality of bargaining power (for example, a confident, professional partner meeting with a less knowledgeable, anxious partner); or
5. where the parties still live under the same roof and negotiations are likely to continue in a more productive manner outside of mediation.

Disclosure of evidence and negotiations can be dealt with by your solicitors, but this can be a lengthy and costly process as letters will be sent between solicitors who will need to meet with you to take instructions at various stages during the process.

By contrast, in mediation you and your former partner have the opportunity to meet together with trained mediators to discuss your options and, hopefully, to reach an agreement. The main advantages of mediation are as follows.

- You and your partner are in control of the process and the timescales.
- Successful mediation is much cheaper than the court process (by a factor of at least ten in most cases).
- The powers of the court tend to be rather inflexible and limited. In mediation, you and your partner are free to reach an agreement that accommodates your own particular circumstances and that best suits you (although it is important to remember that, as with all negotiations, compromise is necessary to settle).
- Experience tells us professionals that mediated agreements tend to last whereas those imposed by the court (particularly where children's arrangements are concerned) often break down.
- The mediator will arrange for disclosure of evidence so that the process will be conducted with 'cards on the table' by both parties (i.e. no nasty surprises along the way).
- The process is privileged, meaning that neither of you can remind the other of concessions or offers made in mediation afterwards (i.e. neither you nor your partner could say in court 'but you agreed to this in mediation' or refer to these discussions in open correspondence). Neither of you will be bound by anything discussed in mediation until you have reached an agreement, which has then been converted by the mediator into a 'memorandum of understanding', which both parties have taken to their own solicitors outside of mediation and signed. Only at that point will any mediated agreement become binding. Therefore, the process has plenty

of safeguards for the parties who are free to discuss ideas and scenarios without fear of repercussions for them.

- Mediation can be tailored to the needs of the parties. So, for example, sessions can be organised on a shuttle basis in separate rooms if there is some discomfort about mediating together. Where there is a concern about safety the mediator can arrange staggered arrival and departure times for the parties. It may also be helpful for you both to be supported by your solicitors throughout the process. This can, in fact, lead to swifter settlements because you both feel more confident to negotiate with on-the-spot access to legal advice. At the end of a successful mediation, the solicitors can prepare the formal agreement. Too often an apparently successful mediation ends with one party having second thoughts because they did not feel confident to reach a settlement without legal advice at the time.
- Parties using the family mediation scheme remain eligible for legal aid to help them with the cost of mediation providing they qualify financially. Even if they don't qualify, the first session is still free for both parties to family mediation. Legal aid costs incurred in mediation will not be repayable (under the 'Statutory Charge') from a settlement reached in mediation.

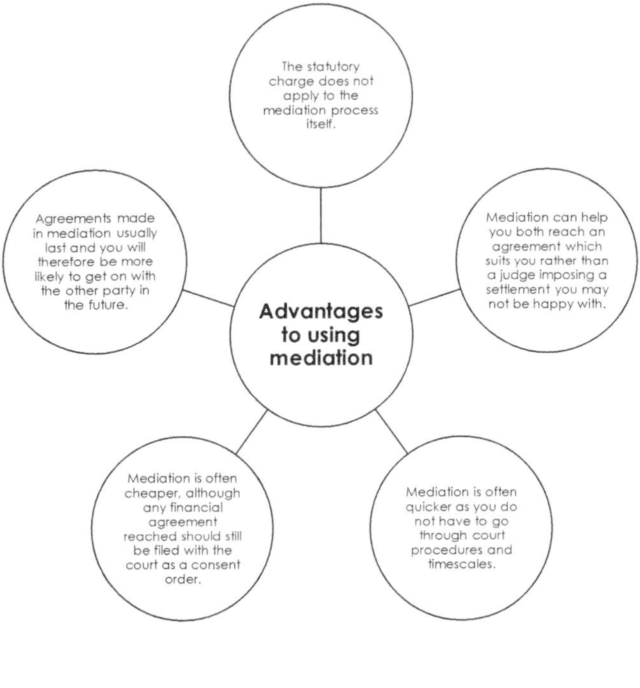

FIGURE 8

The referral process is simple; just call the mediators or specialist providers of ADR and they will help you through the process and explain the cost. Keep a written record of the referral and your opponent's response to it; this may be relevant to the court later.

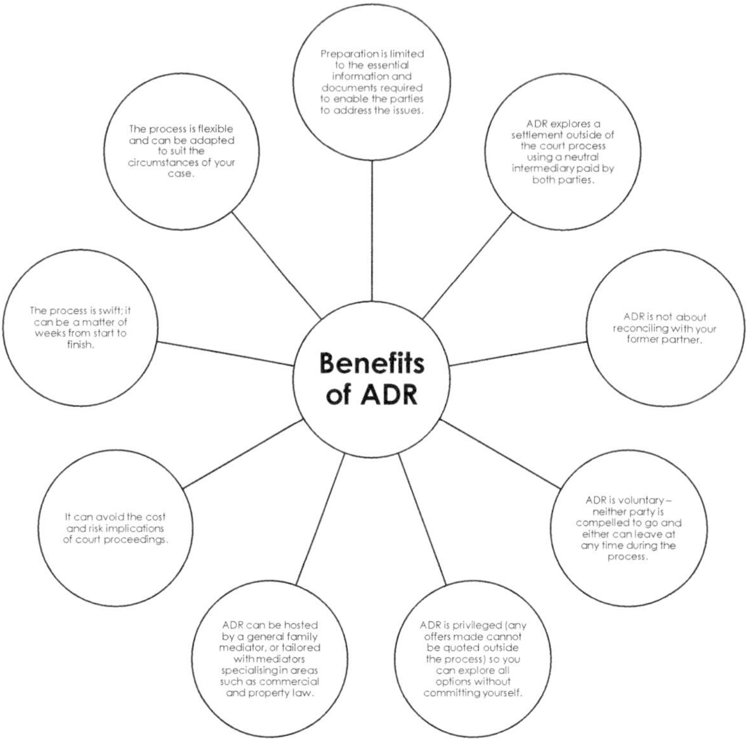

Figure 9

MEDIATION AND CHILDREN DISPUTES

Once the decision to separate has been made, one of the first things to consider are arrangements for the children. There are numerous fears and problems for parents and children to deal with at this difficult time (see Figure 10).

We all want to do the best for our children, but the pressure of trying to cope with this can result in the children getting caught up in our difficulties. Mediation is not an easy option. It can be a painful and demanding process. However, it is vital to explore it because the court process is often very damaging to parental relationships and

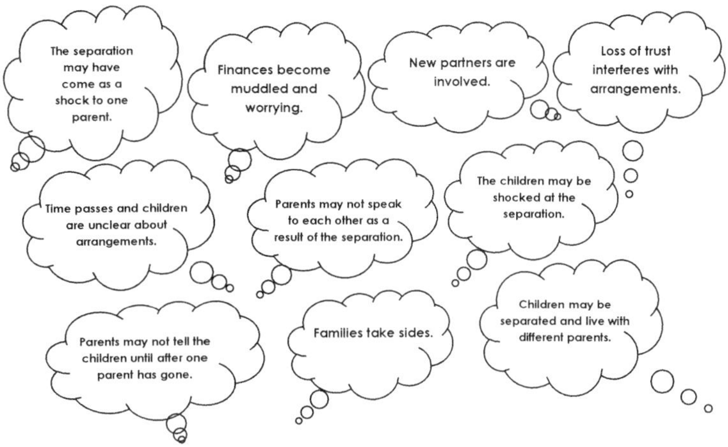

FIGURE 10

any spirit of cooperation which may exist between parents. So too is correspondence between solicitors, which is one of the least effective methods of resolving disputes about the arrangements for your children. It is slow; letters often arrive long after the issue has moved on, often reopening the wounds of the recent conflict. It is also an abdication of the responsibility to hear your former partner's point of view. Worst of all, an excoriating letter from a harassed solicitor will only elicit the same in reply. Most family lawyers subscribe to the principles of an organisation known as Resolution[75] that encourages constructive dialogue but, even so, the written word leaves so much unsaid that a skilled solicitor will still find their carefully crafted correspondence provoking a storm of protest. Mediation is different and can help because, with the help of a trained mediator, you can:

1. Focus on the co-parenting relationship and the shared responsibility for your children's welfare when making plans.
2. Keeps centred on your children's needs and feelings. Mediation keeps us in touch with our children's day-to-day lives, unlike solicitors' correspondence and the court process which can seem remote and disconnected from them.
3. Be swift and responsive to a changing situation. It can be used as a means of putting interim arrangements in place for the children to spend time with you both while you sort out the other issues. You can also bring issues back to mediation more swiftly and cheaply than going to court.

A mediation assessment meeting is now compulsory before applying to the court except in limited circumstances. You have to attend a meeting with a mediator to receive information about alternative ways in which a dispute can be resolved. If, having attended this meeting, you feel mediation is not suitable for you, or if the other party does not attend the mediation appointment, a form will be issued by the mediator. This form will have to be sent to the Court when your application is made. There are only limited cases where mediation is not compulsory.

Costs

The costs of mediation will vary depending on which mediation agency is used, but it usually costs between £140 and £250 per session. Legal aid is available for mediation if you are financially eligible and, if your former partner is eligible but you are not, you may be able to have the first mediation session free.

ARBITRATION

Arbitration differs from mediation. A mediator is a professional who helps the parties to reach agreement whereas an arbitrator is a judge hired privately by the parties in a dispute to decide the case for them. The arbitrator's decison is binding and can be registered and enforced through the civil courts. Court fees have increased enormously since the 2008 credit crunch. The government is generating revenue through the court system to offset the cost of the service. For example, to issue a claim for £200,000 in the civil courts now costs £10,000 with yet more fees to pay during the process. In many cases, it is now so expensive to litigate that it simply isn't worth it. Arbitration is therefore growing in popularity as an alternative to the Court process. The cost varies, but compares favourably with the latest court fees and it is split between the parties.

Arbitration:

- is private (as opposed to open court proceedings);
- is dealt with by a specialist arbitrator chosen by the parties (rather than a different judge for every hearing);
- happens on a date convenient to the parties (rather than being one of many cases in a judge's list);
- is focussed on the issues agreed by the parties in advance;
- uses a procedure agreed in advance by the parties and tailored to their requirements (for example, written representations or limited evidence);
- is binding and can be registered with and enforced through a court;

- can be used to determine various issues including financial arrangements between cohabitees and the arrangements for children.

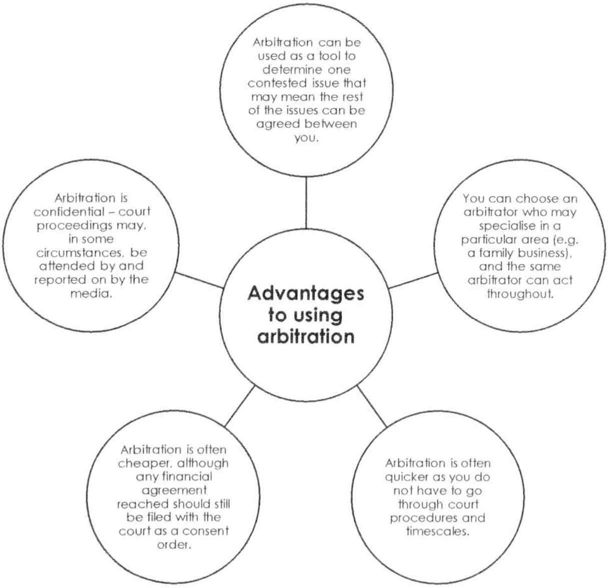

FIGURE 11

Once arbitration has been chosen as a method of resolving a dispute, the successful party can proceed to register the award in the court for enforcement purposes. If either party wants to dispute it they are entitled to do so, and the court may ask them to show a good reason why the arbitrated award should not be reflected in a court order. Issues such as discrimination on grounds of gender or age, or undue influence to agree to the arbitration, may provide a reason why an arbitrated award would not be approved by the court, but where the parties had competent advice and have equal or reasonably equal bargaining power, this would not be done lightly.

NOTES

[74] CPR 44.4 (3) (i) and (ii) refers.
[75] **http://www.resolution.org.uk/**

PART V

WHAT HAPPENS ON DEATH?

◆22◆

Claims on Death and Safeguards

There is still a wide-spread belief that cohabitants are already protected, and this misapprehension is compounded by the fact that such a low proportion of them make a will.[76] The death of a partner is a time of vulnerability for the unmarried, particularly those who have been in a long-term relationship with or are heavily dependent on the deceased. It is an area where simple, inexpensive precautions can be taken to ensure that an unmarried partner is properly provided for in the event of the death of a partner. These precautions will also avoid unpleasant and costly disputes with the deceased's estate or beneficiaries.

It is necessary to distinguish between those who die intestate (i.e. without leaving a will) and those who leave a valid will at the date of their death. An unmarried partner can make provision for their partner by will as they see fit. In a long-term relationship of dependence, particularly one with children, it is wise to consider this, even if you want to make provision for others, because failing to do so may invite a claim against your estate on death.

Thought should be given to your partner's housing and income needs and to those of your children as well as any third parties for whom you wish to provide. It is not unusual for couples with joint property in long-term relationships to make 'mirror' wills so that they each make identical provision for the other on death.

A death intestate means that your (or your unmarried partner's) relatives will inherit in a strict order of priority (see below), which leaves an unmarried partner out in the cold because they do not feature in the categories of persons who will benefit under the intestacy rules, regardless of how deserving an objective third party may think them to be.

Members of the deceased's family who have the right to inherit under the intestacy also have a right to apply for a grant of representation, and the order of entitlement is the same. A person who is lower in the order of entitlement may not apply for the grant unless all living persons with a prior entitlement have renounced their rights to the grant. The right never arises for the deceased's unmarried partner. Full details of the intestacy rules and worked examples can be found at Resource 4. In brief, however, the following is the order of entitlement both to a grant of representation and to inherit:

1. the spouse or civil partner;
2. the children;
3. the parents;
4. the brothers and sisters of the whole blood or their children if the brothers/sisters have died;
5. the brothers and sisters of the half-blood (i.e. they share one parent with the deceased) or their children (as above);
6. the grandparents;
7. the uncles and aunts of the whole blood or their children; and then
8. uncles and aunts of the half-blood or their issue.

If there are no living relatives in any of the above categories, the unmarried partner is still bypassed in favour of the Treasury Solicitor acting for the Crown or the Duchy of Lancaster or the Duchy of Cornwall.

Failure to make adequate provision for a person who is financially dependent on you at the time of your death can result in a claim being made against your estate. The Inheritance (Provision for Family and Dependents) Act 1975 entitles them to do this. The Act permits claims to be made by:

1. Any person (who was not a spouse or same sex civil partner) and who was being maintained (either wholly or partly) by the deceased immediately prior to his death. They may apply to the court for an order if the deceased made inadequate (or no) provision for them by their will or if they are to receive nothing or not enough under the intestacy rules. The test for

whether a person was being 'maintained' by the deceased is that, without expecting any money or anything valuable in return, the deceased was 'making a substantial contribution in money or money's worth to that person's reasonable needs'; or

2. A person who lived in a relationship akin to that of husband and wife[77] in the same household as the deceased during the whole of the period of two years ending immediately before the date of death.

The difference between 1. and 2. above is that category 1. permits a claim by anyone provided they satisfy the test of being maintained by the deceased immediately prior to their death. Category 2. permits an unmarried partner to make a claim without having to prove financial dependence on the deceased (hence the importance of ensuring your unmarried partner is provided for adequately, even if you don't think they are deserving).

As to the circumstances in which a court will conclude that a couple lived together in a relationship akin to husband and wife, we have the comments of Baroness Hale: 'what matters most is the essential quality of the relationship, its marriage-like intimacy, stability, and social and financial inter-dependence'.[78]

As might be imagined, there have been challenges to unmarried claimants on the grounds that relationships have ended before death. This has even extended to situations where the deceased was admitted to hospital shortly prior to death and, consequently, it has been suggested that the deceased and partner were not living together at the time of death. Not surprisingly, the courts have been fairly generous to the (objectively) deserving surviving partners in deciding these issues.[79]

As to what is considered reasonable financial provision, the Act defines it as that which is 'reasonable in all the circumstances of the case for the applicant to receive'. The variation in circumstances is so great that it is impossible to say what that might be. Factors that will be at play include:

1. the financial and other circumstances of the applicant;
2. the nature of their relationship with the deceased and the extent of their dependence on that person;
3. the existence of any other dependents or competing claimants for the estate; and
4. the size of the estate.

Accordingly the range of provision that the estate of a deceased partner might be ordered to make to a surviving partner varies enormously. Take advice if your unmarried partner has died without making any or any adequate provision for you.

Remember, however difficult it is (and when you are grieving, it is going to be tough for you) it is important to act swiftly, because there is a six-month legal limitation period to bring court proceedings[80] once a Grant of Probate (proving the will) has been given or Letters of Administration (for an intestate person's estate) granted. Fortunately it is possible to keep a track of this process using the online probate search facility[81] but bear in mind that the process can take up to ten days in an already short timescale.

Interim orders[82] are possible where, for example, the deceased left an unmarried partner who was wholly dependent upon them and who has an immediate need, and there are sufficient available resources in the estate to provide for the surviving partner.

An alternative to making provision by will is to nominate pension rights for the benefit of your unmarried partner so as to minimise or extinguish their dependency on death.

Reforms to public sector pensions were slow to catch up with the trend of cohabitation, having only been introduced over the period 2002 to 2008. Thankfully, all the main public sector schemes have now introduced discretionary benefits for surviving partners, provided they are able to demonstrate a dependency on the deceased at the time of death or a mutual dependency between the deceased and their partner. The rules have been standardized across the various public schemes.

Every scheme will have its own rules and procedures. By way of a typical example, the guidance issued by the Teacher's Pension Scheme is as follows:

> **Who will receive the death grant?**
> Your spouse, civil partner or nominated partner will automatically receive the death grant unless you've nominated someone else to receive it. If you have nominated a person or persons they will receive the death grant. If you have no spouse, nominated partner or nominee, any payment will be issued to your estate. Please note you're not able to nominate a Trust or Charity to receive the death grant.
>
> **How do I nominate someone?**
> You can complete a nomination via our website or you can ask your employer for a form. If you choose to nominate somebody to receive your death grant it's important to keep it up to date. You can

> nominate more than one person, but if you want to do that you must tell Teachers' Pensions what proportion of the death grant you want each person to receive.

In the private sector, by contrast, the trustees have long had discretion to make provision for surviving unmarried partners. You and your unmarried partner would be well advised to give some thought to this option. Even if you are of the view that you want all or most of your estate to pass to someone other than your partner, if your partner is financially dependent on you and has lived with you for over two years then, as we have seen, they have a potential claim in the event of your death. Making a nomination of all or a proportion of your pension death benefits will discourage any claims because your partner would be financially independent or less dependent on you following the payment of those benefits. This would assist your trustees in resisting any claim made against your estate, so that you would be able to leave all or more of it to the beneficiaries of your choice.

CLAIMS BY A COHABITEE WHERE THEIR PARTNER DIES THROUGH THE FAULT OF OTHERS

The Fatal Accidents Act 1976 permits a claim to be made for bereavement or dependency where, for example, a partner dies through the negligence of some third party such as an employer or a motorist responsible for a road traffic accident in which the partner is killed.

The term 'dependent' includes any person who:

1. was living with the deceased in the same household immediately before the date of the death; and
2. had been living with the deceased in the same household for at least two years before that date; and
3. was living during the whole of that period as the 'husband' or 'wife' of the deceased.

The term also includes any child or other descendent of the deceased

Although a partner (or even an unacknowledged partner can claim if S.1(3) of the Act applies, the requirements relating to claims by cohabitees are onerous. Living in your partner's 'house' is not the same (in law) as living in his or her 'household'. The former implies mere physical presence, while the latter implies a sense of family.

There is also a distinction between 'wanting' to live in the same household, 'intending' to live there, making plans to live there and actually living there.

Section 1.3(4) of the Fatal Accidents Act provides that: 'there shall be taken account (together with any other matter that appears to the Court to be relevant to the action) the fact that the dependant had no enforceable right to financial support by the deceased as a result of their living together'. On a practical level this means that the court might award less to a bereaved cohabitee than to a widow(er) to reflect the perception that the relationship might not have survived as well as a marriage; an assumption that many cohabitees will find insulting.

OTHER DIFFICULTIES CAUSED TO A SURVIVOR ON DEATH

If you are not married or not in a civil partnership and you and your partner have separate bank accounts, neither of you can have access to money held in the other's account. If one of you dies, any funds in the account will become part of the estate and cannot be used until the estate is settled. This can leave the survivor in financial difficulties while matters are sorted out.

If you have a joint account, you both have the right to access the money in the account. Even though you are unmarried or not civil partnered, if one of you should die the whole account would immediately become the property of the other.

Where there are minor children of the relationship being looked after by the surviving parent, the situation is eased for the surviving parent because the children will inherit under the intestacy rules (unless the deceased provided otherwise by his/her will or was still legally married to someone other than the surviving parent at the time of death). However, if the children are still minors, the share of the estate they inherit would have to be held for them by a trustee until they attain majority. A statutory trust arises on death. The assets that will belong to the children pass to the Public Trustee nominally until a grant of representation is issued. In cases of intestacy this is called 'Letters of Administration'. After the grant has been issued the estate is held in trust by the Personal Representatives who have the power to sell the assets. The statutory trust remains in place until all the estate liabilities have been paid and the remaining assets have been distributed.

NOTES

[76] Only 12 per cent in the 2006 British Social Attitudes Survey.

[77] This applies equally to unmarried same sex couples - I(PFD)A 1975 S1 (1A) (b) refers.

[78] *Ghaidan* v. *Godin-Mendoza* [2004] UKHL 30 / [2004] 2 FLR 600.

[79] Re Watson (Deceased) [1999] 1 FLR 878 and *Gully* v. *Dix* [2004] 1 FLR 918, being good examples.

[80] I(PFD)Act 1975 s.4 refers.

[81] **https://www.gov.uk/search-will-probate**

[82] I(PFD)Act 1975 s.5 refers.

RESOURCE 1

Useful Contacts

Government departments

Money Advice Service website - **https://www.moneyadviceservice.org.uk**
Directgov website - **https://www.gov.uk**
Department for Work and Pensions **https://www.gov.uk/government/organisations/department-for-work-pensions**
The Pension Service - **https://www.gov.uk/contact-pension-service**
National Debtline - **https://www.nationaldebtline.org/ (free phone 0808 808 4000)**

Pensioner/carers organisations

Care for Carers - **http://www.careforcarers.org.uk/support/counsel-and-care**
Age UK - **http://www.ageuk.org.uk** (Age UK advice line: 0800 169 6565)

Private pensions

The Financial Conduct Authority and the Prudential Regulation Authority (formerly the Financial Services Authority) can respectively be found at **http://www.fca.org.uk** and **http://www.bankofengland.co.uk/pra/Pages/default.aspx**
The Pensions Regulator - **http://www.thepensionsregulator.gov.uk**
The Pensions Advisory Service - **http://www.pensionsadvisoryservice.org.uk/**

Property ownership

HM Land registry (find out about a property; how much did it cost, is it mortgaged, if so to whom, who has rights affecting it, are there any creditors secured against it, who owns it, in what shares, etc.) - **https://www.gov.uk/government/organisations/land-registry** (Customer Support: 0300 006 0411)

Child support

The Child Support Agency or Child Maintenance Service (information about calculating and collecting child support) - **https://www.gov.uk/child-maintenance/overview** (helpline number 0345 713 3133)

Help to deal with domestic abuse

Gov.UK - **https://www.gov.uk/guidance/domestic-violence-and-abuse**
The National Domestic Violence Helpline- **http://www.nationaldomesticviolencehelpline.org.uk/** (24/7 hotline number 0808 2000 247)
Note: there will be a number of organisations local to you that you can access by contacting the above organisations or by a Google search refined to your locality. Each police force has its own dedicated Domestic Violence Officer who can be contacted through your local constabulary for advice and support.

Legal Aid

Gov.UK (Legal Aid is not easy to obtain any more, but still available in certain circumstances). Find out if you are eligible at - **https://www.gov.uk/legal-aid/overview**

Parenting support (pre- and post-separation)

Mumsnet (great website providing help and support for parents) - **http://www.mumsnet.com**
Families Need Fathers (advice and support for all parents and grandparents who play or hope to play a prominent role in a child's life following parental separation) - **https://fnf.org.uk/**
The Grandparents Association (grandparents are often the voice of reason and a steadying influence in a child's life post-separation. This organisation provides help and support to grandparents who already play a significant role or who believe that they have a greater role to play for the grandchildren) - **http://www.grandparents-association.org.uk**

RESOURCE 2

Parental Responsibility Agreement

Click here to reset form | Click here to print form

Parental Responsibility Agreement
Section 4(1)(b) Children Act 1989

Keep this form in a safe place
Date recorded at The Central Family Court:

Read the notes on the other side before you make this agreement.

This is a Parental Responsibility Agreement regarding

the Child — *Full Name*

Gender — *Date of birth* — *Date of 18th birthday*

Between
the Mother — *Name*

Address

and the Father — *Name*

Address

We declare that — we are the mother and father of the above child and we agree that the child's father shall have parental responsibility for the child (in addition to the mother having parental responsibility).

Signed **(Mother)** — Signed **(Father)**

Date — Date

Certificate of witness

The following evidence of identity was produced by the person signing above: — The following evidence of identity was produced by the person signing above:

Signed in the presence of:
Name of Witness — Signed in the presence of:
Name of Witness

Address — *Address*

Signature of Witness — *Signature of Witness*

[A Justice of the Peace] [Justices' Clerk] [An assistant to a justices' clerk] [An officer of the court authorised by the judge to administer oaths] — [A Justice of the Peace] [Justices' Clerk] [An assistant to a justices' clerk] [An Officer of the Court authorised by the judge to administer oaths]

Notes about the Parental Responsibility Agreement

Read these notes before you make the agreement.

About the Parental Responsibility Agreement

The making of this agreement will affect the legal position of the mother and the father. You should both seek legal advice before you make the Agreement. You can obtain the name and address of a solicitor from the Children Panel (020 7242 1222)

or from

- a local office of the family court
- a Citizens Advice Bureau
- a Law Centre
- a local library.

You may be eligible for legal aid.

When you fill in the Agreement

Please use black ink (the Agreement will be copied). Put the name of one child only. If the father is to have parental responsibility for more than one child, fill in a separate form for each child. **Do not sign the Agreement.**

When you have filled in the Agreement

Take it to a local office of the family court, or The Central Family Court (the address is below).

A justice of the peace, a justices' clerk, an assistant to a justices' clerk, or a court official who is authorised by the judge to administer oaths, will witness your signature and he or she will sign the certificate of the witness. **A solicitor cannot witness your signature.**

To the mother: When you make the declaration you will have to prove that you are the child's mother so take to the court the child's full birth certificate.

You will also need evidence of your identity showing a photograph and signature (for example, a photocard, official pass or passport). **Please note that the child's birth certificate cannot be accepted as sufficient proof of your identity.**

To the father: You will need evidence of your identity showing a photograph and signature (for example, a photocard, official pass or passport).

When the Certificate has been signed and witnessed

Make 2 copies of the Agreement form. You do not need to copy these notes.

Take, or send, this form and the copies to **The Central Family Court, First Avenue House, 42-49 High Holborn, London, WC1V 6NP**.

The Court will record the Agreement and keep this form. The copies will be stamped and sent back to each parent at the address on the Agreement. The Agreement will not take effect until it has been received and recorded at The Central Family Court.

Ending the Agreement

Once a parental responsibility agreement has been made it can only end

- by an order of the court made on the application of any person who has parental responsibility for the child
- by an order of the court made on the application of the child with permission of the court
- when the child reaches the age of 18.

RESOURCE 3

Form JO

Land Registry
Trust Information

JO

Any parts of the form that are not typed should be completed in black ink and in block capitals.

This form may accompany an application in Form AP1, FR1 or ADV1 where:

- panel 9 of Form FR1 or ADV1 has not been completed and the applicant is more than one person, or
- the Form AP1 relates to a transfer (in Form AS1, AS3, TP1, TP2, TR1, TR2 or TR5) or a prescribed clauses lease (within rule 58A of the Land Registration Rules 2003) of a registered estate to more than one person (the Joint Owners), and
  - the declaration of trust panel in the transfer or lease has not been completed and/or the transfer has not been executed by the Joint Owners, and
  - the estate transferred or leased is not a rentcharge, franchise, profit or manor.

Enter the same information as either in the transfer or lease to the Joint Owners or in panel 6 of Form ADV1. Leave blank if this form accompanies a Form FR1.	1	Title number(s) of the property:
Insert address including postcode (if any) or other description of the property as it appears either in the transfer or lease to the Joint Owners, in panel 3 of Form ADV1 or in panel 2 of Form FR1.	2	Property:
	3	Date:
Give full name(s) and address(es), as in either the transfer or lease to the Joint Owners, panels 6 and 7 of Forms ADV1 or panels 6 and 8 of Form FR1.	4	Joint Owners:
Complete either this or panel 6. Place an 'X' in the appropriate box. If completing the fourth box, insert details either of the trust or of the trust instrument under which the Joint Owners hold the property. The registrar will enter a Form A restriction in the register if an 'X' is placed: – in the second or third box, or – in the fourth box, unless it is clear that the Joint Owners hold on trust for themselves alone as joint tenants. If this panel is completed, each Joint Owner must sign. Please refer to Joint property ownership and practice guide 24: private trusts of land for further guidance. These are both available on the GOV.UK website.	5	☐ The Joint Owners declare that they are to hold the property on trust for themselves alone as joint tenants ☐ The Joint Owners declare that they are to hold the property on trust for themselves alone as tenants in common in equal shares ☐ The Joint Owners declare that they hold the property on trust for themselves alone as tenants in common in the following unequal shares: (*complete*) ☐ The Joint Owners are to hold the property (*complete*): Signature of each of the Joint Owners ____________ ____________ Date:

RESOURCE 4

The Intestacy Rules

WHAT ARE THE RULES OF INTESTACY?

When a person dies without leaving a valid will, their property (the estate) must be shared out according to certain rules. These are called the rules of intestacy. A person who dies without leaving a will is called an intestate person.

Only married or civil partners and some other close relatives can inherit under the rules of intestacy.

If someone makes a will but it is not legally valid, the rules of intestacy decide how the estate will be shared out, not the wishes expressed in the will.

Married partners and civil partners

Married partners or civil partners inherit under the rules of intestacy only if they are actually married or in a civil partnership at the time of death. So, if you are divorced or if your civil partnership has been legally ended, you can't inherit under the rules of intestacy. But partners who separated informally can still inherit under the rules of intestacy.

If there are surviving children, grandchildren or great grandchildren of the person who died and the estate is valued at more than £250,000, the partner will inherit:

- all the personal property and belongings of the person who has died, and
- the first £250,000 of the estate, and
- half of the remaining estate.

If there are no surviving children, grandchildren or great-grandchildren, the partner will inherit:

- all the personal property and belongings of the person who has died and
- the whole of the estate with interest from the date of death.

Jointly-owned property

Couples (including the unmarried) may jointly own their home. There are two different ways of jointly owning a home. These are beneficial joint tenancies and tenancies in common.

If the partners were beneficial joint tenants at the time of the death, when the first partner dies the surviving partner will automatically inherit the other partner's share of the property. However, if the partners are tenants in common, the surviving partner does not automatically inherit the other person's share.

Couples may also have joint bank or building society accounts. If one dies, the other partner will automatically inherit the whole of the money.

Property and money that the surviving partner inherits does not count as part of the estate of the person who has died when it is being valued for the intestacy rules.
For example:

> Violet and Arthur are unmarried and own their house jointly as beneficial joint tenants. Arthur is separated from his former wife Betty, but they remain married to one another. Arthur dies intestate leaving the jointly-owned house worth £150,000 and £60,000 in savings in his own name. The house goes automatically to Violet. This leaves an estate of £60,000, which goes to Betty.
> If Arthur had owned the savings jointly with Violet, the savings would have passed to her as well as Arthur's share of the house.
> If Arthur owned the house as well as the savings in his name alone, Betty, as his wife, would inherit both the house and his savings under the intestacy rules. In this scenario, the position would have been no better for Violet even if the estate had been larger and Arthur had been unmarried, because of the order in which first blood relatives then relatives by marriage inherit under the intestacy rules (see below). Violet would inherit nothing and would have to seek some financial provision from Arthur's estate through the courts (see below).

Close relatives

Children

Children of the intestate person will inherit if there is no surviving married partner. If there is a surviving married partner, they will inherit only if the estate is worth more than a certain amount.

Children - if there is no surviving married or civil partner

If there is no surviving married partner, the children of a person who has died without leaving a will inherit the whole estate. This applies however much the estate is worth. If there are two or more children, the estate will be divided equally between them.

Children - if there is a surviving partner

If there is a surviving married partner, a child only inherits from the estate if the estate is valued at over £250,000. If there are two or more children, the children will inherit one half of the value of the estate above £250,000 in equal shares.

All the children of the parent who has died intestate inherit equally from the estate. This also applies where a parent has children from different relationships.

For example:

> Bill and Davina are divorced. They have three children. Bill now lives in an unmarried relationship with Scarlett and they have a child Anna. Bill dies. Neither Davina nor Scarlett will inherit from Bill under the Intestacy Rules because they are not married to Bill. The four children inherit Bill's estate in equal shares. If Davina's claims on divorce have not been dismissed by a court she can make a claim against Bill's estate under the Inheritance (Provision for Family and Dependents) Act 1975. Scarlett can also claim under the same statute provided she and Bill had been living together for at least two years prior to Bill's death. What an unfortunate situation. Davina, Scarlett and the children would be in dispute with one another over Bill's estate.

A child whose parents are not married or have not registered a civil partnership can inherit from the estate of a parent who dies intestate. These children can also inherit from grandparents or great-grandparents who have died intestate.

Adopted children (including step-children who have been adopted by their step-parent) have rights to inherit under the rules of intestacy. But otherwise you have to be a biological child to inherit.

Children do not receive their inheritance immediately. They receive it when they:

- reach the age of 18, or
- marry or form a civil partnership under this age.

Until then, trustees manage the inheritance on their behalf.

Grandchildren and great grandchildren

A grandchild or great grandchild cannot inherit from the estate of an intestate person unless either:

- their parent or grandparent has died before the intestate person, or
- their parent is alive when the intestate person dies but dies before reaching the age of 18 without having married or formed a civil partnership.

In these circumstances, the grandchildren and great grandchildren will inherit equal shares of the share to which their parent or grandparent would have been entitled.

Other close relatives

Parents, brothers and sisters and nieces and nephews of the intestate person may inherit under the rules of intestacy. This will depend on a number of circumstances:

- whether there is a surviving married or civil partner;
- whether there are children, grandchildren or great grandchildren;
- in the case of nephews and nieces, whether the parent directly related to the person who has died is also dead;
- the amount of the estate.

Other relatives may have a right to inherit if the person who died intestate had no surviving married partner or civil partner, children, grandchildren, great grand-children, parents, brothers, sisters, nephews or nieces. The order of priority among other relatives is as follows:

- grandparents;
- uncles and aunts - a cousin can inherit instead if the uncle or aunt who would have inherited died before the intestate person;
- half-uncles and half-aunts - a half-cousin can inherit instead if the half-uncle or half-aunt who would have inherited died before the intestate person.

Who cannot inherit

The following people have no right to inherit where someone dies without leaving a will:

- unmarried partners;
- lesbian or gay partners not in a civil partnership;
- relations by marriage;
- close friends;
- carers.

However, even if you can't inherit under the rules of intestacy, you may be able to apply to court for financial provision from the estate.

If there are no surviving relatives

If there are no surviving relatives who can inherit under the rules of intestacy, the estate passes to the Crown. This is known as *bona vacantia*. The Treasury Solicitor is then responsible for dealing with the estate. The Crown can make grants from the estate but does not have to agree to them.

If you are not a surviving relative, but you believe you have a good reason to apply for a grant, you will need legal advice.

Rearranging the way the estate is shared out

It is possible to rearrange the way property is shared out when someone dies without leaving a will, provided this is done within two years of the death. This is called 'making a deed of family arrangement or variation'. All the people who would inherit under the rules of intestacy must agree.

If they agree, the property can be shared out in a different way so that people who do not inherit under the intestacy rules can still get some of the estate. Or they could agree that the amount that people get is different to the amount they would get under the rules of intestacy.

If you think that the way the estate is shared out should be rearranged, you will need legal advice.

RESOURCE 5

Form TR1

Land Registry
Transfer of whole of registered title(s)

TR1

Any parts of the form that are not typed should be completed in black ink and in block capitals.

If you need more room than is provided for in a panel, and your software allows, you can expand any panel in the form. Alternatively use continuation sheet CS and attach it to this form.

Leave blank if not yet registered.	1 Title number(s) of the property:
Insert address including postcode (if any) or other description of the property, for example 'land adjoining 2 Acacia Avenue'.	2 Property:
	3 Date:
Give full name(s) of **all** the persons transferring the property. Complete as appropriate where the transferor is a company.	4 Transferor: For UK incorporated companies/LLPs Registered number of company or limited liability partnership including any prefix: For overseas companies (a) Territory of incorporation: (b) Registered number in the United Kingdom including any prefix:
Give full name(s) of **all** the persons to be shown as registered proprietors. Complete as appropriate where the transferee is a company. Also, for an overseas company, unless an arrangement with Land Registry exists, lodge either a certificate in Form 7 in Schedule 3 to the Land Registration Rules 2003 or a certified copy of the constitution in English or Welsh, or other evidence permitted by rule 183 of the Land Registration Rules 2003.	5 Transferee for entry in the register: For UK incorporated companies/LLPs Registered number of company or limited liability partnership including any prefix: For overseas companies (a) Territory of incorporation: (b) Registered number in the United Kingdom including any prefix:
Each transferee may give up to three addresses for service, one of which must be a postal address whether or not in the UK (including the postcode, if any). The others can be any combination of a postal address, a UK DX box number or an electronic address.	6 Transferee's intended address(es) for service for entry in the register:
	7 The transferor transfers the property to the transferee

Guidance	Panel
Place 'X' in the appropriate box. State the currency unit if other than sterling. If none of the boxes apply, insert an appropriate memorandum in panel 11.	8 Consideration ☐ The transferor has received from the transferee for the property the following sum (in words and figures): ☐ The transfer is not for money or anything that has a monetary value ☐ Insert other receipt as appropriate:
Place 'X' in any box that applies. Add any modifications.	9 The transferor transfers with ☐ full title guarantee ☐ limited title guarantee
Where the transferee is more than one person, place 'X' in the appropriate box. Complete as necessary. The registrar will enter a Form A restriction in the register *unless*: – an 'X' is placed: – in the first box, or – in the third box and the details of the trust or of the trust instrument show that the transferees are to hold the property on trust for themselves alone as joint tenants, *or* – it is clear from completion of a form JO lodged with this application that the transferees are to hold the property on trust for themselves alone as joint tenants. Please refer to Joint property ownership and practice guide 24: private trusts of land for further guidance. These are both available on the GOV.UK website.	10 Declaration of trust. The transferee is more than one person and ☐ they are to hold the property on trust for themselves as joint tenants ☐ they are to hold the property on trust for themselves as tenants in common in equal shares ☐ they are to hold the property on trust:
Insert here any required or permitted statement, certificate or application and any agreed covenants, declarations and so on.	11 Additional provisions

The transferor must execute this transfer as a deed using the space opposite. If there is more than one transferor, all must execute. Forms of execution are given in Schedule 9 to the Land Registration Rules 2003. If the transfer contains transferee's covenants or declarations or contains an application by the transferee (such as for a restriction), it must also be executed by the transferee.

If there is more than one transferee and panel 10 has been completed, each transferee must also execute this transfer to comply with the requirements in section 53(1)(b) of the Law of Property Act 1925 relating to the declaration of a trust of land. Please refer to *Joint property ownership* and practice guide *24: private trusts of land* for further guidance.

12 Execution

WARNING
If you dishonestly enter information or make a statement that you know is, or might be, untrue or misleading, and intend by doing so to make a gain for yourself or another person, or to cause loss or the risk of loss to another person, you may commit the offence of fraud under section 1 of the Fraud Act 2006, the maximum penalty for which is 10 years' imprisonment or an unlimited fine, or both.

Failure to complete this form with proper care may result in a loss of protection under the Land Registration Act 2002 if, as a result, a mistake is made in the register.

Under section 66 of the Land Registration Act 2002 most documents (including this form) kept by the registrar relating to an application to the registrar or referred to in the register are open to public inspection and copying. If you believe a document contains prejudicial information, you may apply for that part of the document to be made exempt using Form EX1, under rule 136 of the Land Registration Rules 2003.

RESOURCE 6

Request to health professional for medical evidence of injuries/condition consistent with domestic violence

This example letter has been designed by the Ministry of Justice to be used to request evidence of injuries/condition consistent with domestic violence from a doctor (including GP), nurse, midwife, practitioner psychologist or health visitor.

Information required is highlighted and instructions are italicised. ***Please delete any unnecessary text and instructions (including this introduction) before sending.***

[Name of health professional]
[Address of surgery/hospital]

[Your Address]

[Your E-mail (if applicable)]

[Your Contact telephone number]

Dear [insert name of doctor, nurse, practitioner psychologist, health visitor or midwife],

Request for evidence of domestic violence for access to legal aid

I would like your help so I can get Legal Aid.

I would like to request written confirmation that I was examined by you in the last 24 months with injuries or a condition that were consistent with those of a victim of domestic violence. In the event of your being absent, I would be grateful if a medical colleague[1] with access to my medical records could do so.

This is needed as evidence of domestic violence in order that I can access legal aid for a family dispute in accordance with the Legal Aid, Sentencing & Punishment of Offenders Act 2012. Without evidence I will be unable to get legal aid to pursue my family case. **I would therefore be grateful if this could be treated as a matter of urgency.**

There is an example letter for this which is available on www.justice.gov.uk/legal-aid-for-private-family-matters which can be pasted onto the practice/hospital letterhead.

I will then take your letter to a family lawyer so they can assist me with my dispute.

The legal aid legislation defines domestic violence as "any incident, or pattern of incidents, of controlling, coercive or threatening behaviour, violence or abuse (whether psychological, physical, sexual, financial or emotional) between individuals who are associated with each other." This follows the cross-Government definition.

The Ministry of Justice and the Legal Aid Agency recognise that the great majority of physical injuries and many non-physical conditions could be caused by domestic violence.

[1] In order to meet the requirements to access legal aid, this will need to be a doctor, nurse, health visitor, midwife or practitioner psychologist.

I can confirm that the [injuries/condition] that I presented to you with on [insert date when you were examined by the health professional if known] were caused by domestic violence.

[Delete following paragraph if not sending this letter to a GP]

I would be grateful if you could let me know when the letter is ready to collect from the surgery. The best way to contact me is [Enter details on best way to be contacted]

Yours [faithfully/sincerely],

[Add your name here]

RESOURCE 7

Request to Social Services for evidence of an assessment of child abuse or a child protection plan

This example letter has been designed by the Ministry of Justice to request evidence of an assessment of child abuse or a child protection plan.

Information required is highlighted and instructions are italicised. ***Please delete any unnecessary text and instructions (including this introduction) before sending.***

[Social Worker (insert name of Social Worker if known)]
[Social Services Address]

[Your Address]

[Your E-mail (if applicable)]

[Your Contact telephone number]

To whom it may concern [Insert name of Social Worker if known],

[Select one of the following two paragraphs and delete as appropriate]

I would like to request written confirmation that [insert child's name] has been assessed in the last 24 months by social services as at risk or being a victim of abuse by [insert perpetrator's name].

or

I would like to request written confirmation that [insert child's name] has had a child protection plan in the last 24 months put in place to protect [him/her] from abuse by [insert perpetrator's name].

This is needed as evidence of child abuse in order that I can access legal aid for a private children's case in accordance with the Legal Aid, Sentencing & Punishment of Offenders Act 2012. **I would therefore be grateful if this could be treated as a matter of urgency.**

I would be grateful if you could send your written confirmation to [state address where you wish this to be sent].

More information and guidance about the evidential requirements for legal aid in family matters can be found at www.justice.gov.uk/legal-aid-for-private-family-matters. This includes a template letter that you can use to reply.

Yours [faithfully/sincerely],

[Add your name here]

LA.CA.Re.SS.RO_0413

RESOURCE 8

Your Home, Your Assets and Your Residential Care or Nursing Home Fees

If you plan ahead, you can make sure you still have something of value left to leave in your will. There are also ways to avoid selling your home, in case your condition improves and you want to live there again. If you have to spend some time in a residential care or nursing home, you will have to pay part of your fees. However, this doesn't always mean that you will have to sell your home and other assets. You can get information about your options below.

CAPITAL RULES ON CONTRIBUTION TO NURSING HOME FEES

Your capital will be assessed according to the information in the following table:

Over £23,250	You will be assessed as being able to meet the full cost of your care.
Between £14,250 and £23,250	Capital between these amounts will be calculated as providing you with an income of £1 per week for every £250 of your savings.
£14,250 or under	Your capital will be ignored in calculating how much you have to contribute to the cost of your care.

If you own your home then it will usually be counted as capital 12 weeks after you move permanently into a care home. The value of your own home will not be counted as capital if certain close relatives still live there. They are:

- your husband, wife, partner or civil partner;
- a close relative who is 60 or over, or incapacitated;
- a close relative under the age of 16 who you're legally liable to support;
- your ex-husband, ex-wife, ex-civil partner or ex-partner if they are a lone parent.

The local Trust may choose not to count your home as capital in other circumstances - for example, if your carer lives there.

YOUR HOME AND TEMPORARY STAYS IN A RESIDENTIAL CARE OR NURSING HOME

If you go into a residential care or nursing home temporarily, you will have to contribute to the cost. You may not receive a full financial assessment for the first eight weeks, in which case the Health and Social Care Trust will determine a fair contribution for you to make.

For the next four weeks, a financial assessment will be made to determine what you should pay. As your stay is temporary, your home won't be counted as capital.

KEEPING YOUR HOME AND ASSETS

Setting up a family trust is one way of transferring the ownership of your home or other assets to someone else while you're still alive. You should get advice from a solicitor on this because the law surrounding trusts is complicated. A trust specific to the needs of yourself and your family will be required and is beyond the scope of this work.

GIVING MONEY OR PROPERTY TO OTHER PEOPLE

You may choose to give money or assets to your children or grandchildren. There is no monetary limit on gifts to your children, grandchildren or other relatives, but they may have to pay tax on any interest or income they receive.

If you give an asset to someone within the seven years before you die, the person who receives the gift may have to pay Inheritance Tax on it. It is against the law to transfer ownership of an asset to another person specifically to avoid paying your care home fees.

There is no time limit as to how far back a Trust can go to find out if you have given away assets to avoid paying care costs.

If this is found to have happened, the Trust can treat you as if you still had the asset and you will have to pay for your care accordingly. However, the more time that has elapsed between the gifting of assets and the need for care, the more difficult it will be for the Trust to conclude or prove that the gift was made with the specific intention of avoiding the requirement to pay.

If the transfer was within six months of you needing care, the Trust can recover the cost of your care from the person(s) who received the gift. In other words, it will be presumed that the intention behind the transfer was to avoid payment of the fees.

RESOURCE 9

Property: Forms of Ownership and Rental

FORMS OF OWNERSHIP

The single most significant purchase any cohabiting couple will make during their relationship is their home. It is important therefore to understand the various forms of ownership. Broadly they are as follows.

1. Freehold

Freehold, as the name suggests, is the right to hold a parcel of land (including any buildings standing on the land) for an indefinite period (effectively forever).

2. Leasehold

A leasehold property is held for a fixed term. Effectively, a lease is the right to occupy land owned (freehold) by someone else for a term of years. The term varies, but is usually granted for a substantial term such as 99 or 125 years. The value of the lease reduces over time, but particularly as the term reduces to the point where a mortgage lender is less likely to lend or the term will expire during the holder's lifetime. Mortgage lenders don't like to grant mortgages if the remaining term of the lease is less than 50 years because most mortgages are payable over lengthy terms and the value of a shorter lease is less likely to cover the mortgage owing if the borrower fails to pay in the future.

3. Shared equity

Raising a mortgage sufficient to purchase a property in today's market is a real problem, particularly for younger buyers. For this reason, schemes have been developed by 'not for profit' organisations known as Housing Associations[1]. Shared equity means that the purchaser buys a share of the equity either outright in cash, or part cash and part mortgage. The remainder is owned by the Housing Association for which the buyer pays a rent at an affordable rate in addition to paying the monthly mortgage to the lender. The benefits of shared equity are:

1. It provides security of tenure (you can stay for as long as you pay your rent and mortgage and observe the term of the tenancy and mortgage agreement);
2. Those who don't earn enough to raise a mortgage to buy outright can still get on the property ladder by purchasing as much of the property as they can afford;
3. Because Housing Associations are Registered Social Landlords and operate on a 'not for profit' basis, rents are reasonable and terms are fair.

PRIVATE RENTAL OPTIONS

For those who are not able, for whatever reason, to afford to buy or part buy/part rent a property, the other option is to rent. Private sector rental agreements differ from leases in that they are generally for much shorter periods. With few exceptions now, the most commonly used form of tenancy is the Assured Shorthold Tenancy ('AST'). This can be used for houses and flats (i.e. self-contained units) and provides for a tenancy initially for a secure period of six months. This is the most usual form of tenancy which will be offered by private sector landlords.

An Assured Shorthold Tenancy will automatically continue as a statutory periodic tenancy after the end of the contractual fixed term. In other words, the tenancy will run from month to month after the term expires. Once the tenancy becomes 'periodic' it can be ended at any time after service of a properly drafted 'section 21' notice informing the tenant that the landlord requires possession of the property. During the protected six-month period of the tenancy, the landlord has more limited opportunities to end the tenancy. This applies in the event of arrears of rent or a breach of the terms of the tenancy agreement (for example, causing a nuisance, non-payment of rent, damaging the property), in which case the landlord will have to serve the relevant notice on the tenant before taking the matter to court if the tenant fails to rectify the problem. The Housing Act lays down the notice period before the tenant has to deliver possession of the property. If, for whatever reason, the tenant fails to leave at the end of the notice period, the landlord has to take the tenant to court for an order for possession.

Any deposit paid by the tenant must be protected under one of the Government-approved tenancy deposit schemes, which means that the deposit is protected pending the end of the tenancy. The deposit is paid as protection for the landlord against damage to the property or arrears of rent and may be subject to deduction accordingly.

Housing Association tenancies

Housing associations offer similar types of housing as local councils – often to people on a low income or who need extra support.

You can apply directly to a housing association and often through your local council, at which point you will be put on a waiting list. You can apply to more than one housing association at a time.

Housing associations normally offer housing to people most suited to that particular property. You may have to wait a long time for a suitable property to become available.

Types of Housing Association tenancies

Starter tenancy

New housing association tenants may be offered a starter tenancy. These usually last 12 months and are like a 'trial' period.

You become an assured or fixed-term tenant after 12 months, unless your housing association has either started action to evict you or extended your starter tenancy.

Assured and fixed-term tenancies

At the end of your starter tenancy you'll be offered either:

- an assured tenancy - meaning you can normally live in your property for the rest of your life; or
- a fixed-term tenancy - usually lasting for at least five years (your landlord will decide whether it's renewed).

Your rights may include:

- buying your home;
- having your home repaired; and
- swapping your home with another council or housing association tenant.

Ending your tenancy

Your tenancy can be ended if:

- you give the housing association four weeks' notice in writing;
- the housing association evicts you;
- you transfer your tenancy to someone else or swap homes; or
- the housing association needs to move you (for example, to redevelop your property) – in which case it should offer you a new property.

Local Authority housing

You apply through your local council (provided you are over 18, and in some cases over 16). You may be able to apply even if you don't live in the area. Each council has its own rules.

Waiting lists

On applying you will join a waiting list. Waiting times vary from one council area to another. The decision on whether to offer housing or not is made based on a 'points' or 'banding' system.

Points and bands are based on housing need. For example, you're likely to be offered housing first if you:

- are homeless;
- live in cramped conditions; or
- have a medical condition made worse by your current home.

Once you're high enough on the list, your council will contact you about an available property.

Choice-based lettings

Some councils have a choice-based letting scheme. This lets you tell your council which properties you're interested in. It depends on the council but, once you have been accepted onto the waiting list, the basic steps are as follows.

1. Find a property: check in local papers, on council websites, in council offices or in local libraries.
2. Check you can apply for it: some properties are only suitable for single people, families or disabled people.
3. Apply: this is known as 'bidding', but it does not involve money. You can bid online, by phone or by text.
4. Get the council's decision.

Getting an offer

Normally you only have a short time to accept a housing offer. If you don't accept it, you can usually stay on the waiting list (or bid for other properties), but you may be put lower down the list and you may be taken off the list temporarily if you keep rejecting offers.

You can appeal if you're not happy with your council's decision.

Types of council tenancy

Introductory tenancy

New council tenants may be offered an introductory tenancy. These usually last 12 months and are like a 'trial' period.

You automatically become a secure or flexible tenant after 12 months, unless your council has either started action to evict you or extended your introductory tenancy for a further six months.

There are limits to what you can do with an introductory tenancy, for example you can't:

- make major improvements to the property;
- swap your property with another council tenant; or
- apply to buy your property through the Right to Buy scheme.

Secure tenancy

As a secure tenant, you can normally live in the property for the rest of your life, as long as you don't break the conditions of the tenancy.

You can:

- rent out rooms - but you can't sub-let the whole property;
- buy your property through the Right to Buy scheme;
- swap your home with another council or housing association tenant - with your council's permission;
- transfer your tenancy to someone else in some circumstances; and
- make improvements to your home – you will need permission from your council for some types of work.

Flexible tenancy

As a flexible tenant, you have tenancy for a fixed period. This is usually for at least five years, though in some cases it may be between two and five years.

At the end of the fixed period the council may decide to:

- offer you another fixed-term tenancy;

- offer you a secure tenancy; or
- not renew your tenancy.

They must explain their reasons if they decide not to renew your tenancy and give you a chance to challenge the decision.

As a flexible tenant you can:

- rent out rooms - but you can't sub-let the whole property;
- buy your property through the Right to Buy scheme;
- swap your home with another council or housing association tenant - with your council's permission; and
- transfer your tenancy to someone else in some circumstances.

Joint tenancy

Under a joint tenancy, all the tenants share equal responsibility.

You can apply for a joint tenancy at any time if you're married or in a registered civil partnership. You must usually have lived together at the property for at least 12 months if you're a cohabiting couple or related (for example, brother and sister).

Transferring your tenancy

Secure and flexible tenants may be able to transfer a tenancy to someone else or, in some circumstances, pass on a tenancy to someone when they die.

Secure tenancies granted before 1 April 2012 can be transferred or passed on only once. For example, if you take over a tenancy when someone dies, you can't pass on the tenancy to someone else when you die.

Some secure and flexible tenancies granted from 1 April 2012 may mean you can transfer or pass on your tenancy more than once - check your tenancy agreement.

To transfer a tenancy, complete a 'request to assign tenancy' form, available from your local council's housing department.

Ending your tenancy

Your tenancy can only be ended if:

- you give the council four weeks' notice in writing;
- the council evicts you; or
- the council needs to move you (for example, to redevelop the property), in which case it should offer you a new property and a new tenancy with no less security.

Secure tenancies can also end if:

- the council needs to move you (for example, to redevelop your property), in which case it should offer you a new property and a new secure tenancy; or
- you transfer your tenancy to someone else or swap homes.

Ending joint tenancies

If only one of you wants to end the tenancy and the other joint tenant(s) wants to stay in the property, your council may:

- give the remaining tenant(s) a new tenancy at the same property; or
- not give them a new tenancy (for example, because the property could be offered to another couple or family).

If one joint tenant dies, the tenancy continues for the surviving tenant(s).

In the event of separation, there are various remedies that ought to be considered. In particular, as an unmarried partner, you should consider whether you wish to retain the tenancy of the property you share with your partner. If so, consider initially the remedies discussed in Chapter 20 concerning occupation orders. You should also consider whether your partner may attempt to surrender the tenancy and, if so, whether your landlord would be likely to accept such a notice. If you have a chequered history with your landlord, they are more likely to take the opportunity to end the tenancy if one tenant serves notice which they can accept. In the case of Local Authority (council) tenancies, particularly probationary tenancies, one tenant may want to give notice out of spite or to improve their own chances of qualifying for a tenancy elsewhere. Always check with your landlord and inform them that you do not intend to give notice, even if your partner attempts to do so. Most are prepared to hold the tenancy open in those circumstances but, if a particular landlord is not, the party who wishes to retain the tenancy has the right to apply to the court for an order restraining the other from serving notice to end the tenancy.

You may also apply for a transfer of the tenancy to you. This is done using Schedule 7 to the Family Law Act 1996[2] which grants the court the power to order a transfer of various kinds of tenancy as between married and unmarried former partners. The court must take various factors into account including the suitability of each party as a tenant.

NOTES

[1] **https://www.gov.uk/housing-association-homes/apply-for-a-home**

[2] **http://www.legislation.gov.uk/ukpga/1996/27/schedule/7**

RESOURCE 10

Inheritance Tax and Settled Property

Please note that trust law is complex and advice will vary from one individual to the next depending on circumstances. It is essential to seek legal and taxation advice specific to your own circumstances before setting up any form of trust. The following is therefore necessarily no more than a statement of general principles.

The act of putting an asset - such as money, land or buildings - into a trust is often known as 'making a settlement'.

For Inheritance Tax purposes, each asset has its own separate identity so, for example, one asset within a trust may be for the trustees to use at their discretion. Another item within the same trust may be for a disabled person. There will be different Inheritance Tax rules for each asset.

Different assets may receive different tax treatment. It is the total value of all the assets in a trust that is used to work out whether a trust exceeds the Inheritance Tax threshold and whether Inheritance Tax is due.

Inheritance Tax may be due on the assets held within a trust when they are transferred out of a trust (exit charges) or on the 10th anniversary, the only exceptions being assets:

- in an 'interest in possession' trust if put there before 22 March 2006;
- subject to a 'transitional serial interest' made between 22 March 2006 and 5 October 2008;
- put into an 'interest in possession' trust by the terms of a will or the rules of intestacy;
- set aside for a disabled person;
- set aside for a bereaved minor;
- put into an age '18 to 25 trust'.

TRANSFERS INTO TRUST

A transfer of assets into a trust can include buildings, land or money and can be either of the following:

- a gift made during a person's life;
- a transfer or transaction that reduces the value of the settlor's estate (for example, an asset is sold to trustees at less than its market value) - the loss to the person's estate is considered a gift or transfer.

HOW TO WORK OUT IF INHERITANCE TAX IS DUE

For most types of trust Inheritance Tax is due when you make transfers that total more than the Inheritance Tax threshold of £325,000 (note, however, that the present government (2016) is committed to changing this). You work this out by adding up the value of any transfers (based on the loss in value to the settlor's estate) and any chargeable gifts made in the previous seven years by the settlor. Inheritance Tax is due on everything above the threshold. If the trustees pay, the rate of tax is 20 per cent. If the settlor pays the Inheritance Tax instead of the trustee, this means there will be an increased loss from the settlor's estate. The amount of tax due will therefore increase. These calculations are complex.

Death within seven years of making a transfer

If you die within seven years of making a transfer into a trust your estate will have to pay Inheritance Tax at the full amount of 40 per cent. This is instead of the reduced amount of 20 per cent which is payable when the payment is made during your lifetime.

In this case your personal representative - who manages your estate when you die - will have to pay a further 20 per cent out of your estate based on the value of the original transfer.

If no Inheritance Tax was due when you made the transfer, the value of the transfer is added to your estate when working out whether any Inheritance Tax is due.

If you make a gift into any type of trust but continue to benefit from the gift (for example, you give away your house but continue to live in it) you will pay 20 per cent on the transfer and the gift will still count as part of your estate. These are known as gifts 'with reservation of benefit'.

This creates a situation where there are two possible Inheritance Tax charges if you die:

- a charge when you transfer the gift into a trust;
- a charge to your estate when you die - because the asset is still considered part of your estate.

To avoid double taxation, only the higher of these charges is applied - in other words you won't ever pay more than 40 per cent Inheritance Tax.

Gifts into a trust for someone who is disabled

You don't have to pay Inheritance Tax immediately if you make a gift to a trust for someone who is disabled but Inheritance Tax may still be due when you die.

The Inheritance Tax exit charge

Inheritance Tax is charged up to a maximum of six per cent on assets - such as money, land or buildings - transferred out of a trust. This is known as an 'exit charge' and it's charged on all transfers of relevant property.

Transfers out of trust

A transfer out of trust can occur when:
- the trust comes to an end;
- some of the assets within the trust are distributed to beneficiaries;
- a beneficiary becomes 'absolutely entitled' to enjoy an asset;
- an asset becomes part of a 'special trust' (for example, a charitable trust or trust for a disabled person) and it ceases to be 'relevant property';
- the trustees enter into a non-commercial transaction that reduces the value of the trust fund.

When there isn't an Inheritance Tax exit charge

There are some occasions when there is no Inheritance Tax exit charge - these apply even where the trust is a 'relevant property' trust. For instance, it isn't charged:
- on payments by trustees of costs or expenses incurred on assets held as relevant property;
- on some payments of capital to the beneficiary where Income Tax will be due;
- when the asset is transferred out of the trust within three months of setting up a trust, or within three months following a 10-year anniversary;
- when assets are 'excluded property' – some foreign property is 'excluded property'.

The 10 year anniversary charge

As a trustee, you'll have to pay a charge on every tenth anniversary of the date your trust was set up if your trust contains relevant property with a value above the Inheritance Tax threshold.

Work out the Inheritance Tax

Inheritance Tax is charged at each ten-year anniversary of the trust. It's charged on the net value of any relevant property in the trust on the day before that anniversary. Net value is the value after deducting any debts and reliefs.

DEALING WITH A TRUST WHEN SOMEONE DIES

When someone dies, the job of managing their estate may involve dealing with trusts.

The deceased may have wanted their assets put into trust when they die, or part of their estate may have already been held in trust.

The executor or administrator of the deceased's estate - known as the 'personal representative' - must find out the total value of the estate.

Inheritance Tax is due on everything above the Inheritance Tax threshold (£325,000 for the tax year 2015 to 2016). This can become more complicated when a trust is involved.

There are three main ways that the deceased's personal representative may have to deal with a trust when working out whether Inheritance Tax is due.

When the deceased was the beneficiary of a trust

Some trusts are set up so that the beneficiary has ownership or a legal right to the income or assets in the trust. This will affect what's included in the estate of the beneficiary when they die.

A bare trust is one where the beneficiary is entitled to both the income and the assets in the trust. Therefore, when they die, both income and assets are considered part of their estate. The personal representative needs to work out whether there is any Inheritance Tax to pay and include the deceased's interest in the bare trust.

An interest in possession trust is one where the beneficiary is entitled to only the income from a trust. When they die, there are certain circumstances where the value of this 'interest in possession' is calculated as part of their estate.

When the deceased transferred assets into a trust before they died

There may have been an Inheritance Tax charge of 20 per cent when assets were transferred into a trust. If you're the personal representative you must find out whether the deceased made any transfers into a trust in the seven years before they died. If they did, and they paid Inheritance Tax at that time, the tax will be recalculated at 40 per cent and a credit allowed for the tax paid when the trust was set up. The trustees will be liable to pay the extra tax.

When a trust is set up by a will

Someone might ask in their will that, when they die, some or all of their assets are placed in a trust. A trust set up under these circumstances is known as a 'will trust'. The personal representative must then make sure that the trust is set up properly and all taxes are paid on assets going into it.

Deadlines, penalties and payments

If the chargeable event occurred on or after 6 April 2014, trustees must pay Inheritance Tax by the end of the sixth month after the event. The trustee must also report the event to HMRC by the end of the sixth month after it happened. HMRC will charge interest on payments.

Index

ND - #0100 - 110926 - C0 - 216/138/12 - PB - 9781910226483 - Gloss Lamination